THE BOY
THE TREE &
THE TRENCH

AN AUTOBIOGRAPHY

THE BOY
THE TREE &
THE TRENCH

Dr. Dave Poulton, Ph. D

TIFFANY HOUSE
Australia

Copyright 2022 © Dr. Dave Poulton Ph.D

All rights reserved. No part of this book is to be reproduced by any means, electronic, including photocopying or by any information storage retrieval system without the written permission of the author.

Cover design George Mousse

Because of the dynamic nature of the Internet, any web addresses or links contained in this book may have changed since publication and may no longer be valid.

The author has taken every effort to contact some out-of-town people. If you see the relevancy of this note, could you please contact the author.

Scripture taken from the New King James Version copyright 1982 by Thomas Nelson Inc. Used by permission. All rights reserved.

ISBN 978-1-922541-12-3

ISBN 978-1-9-22541-

National Library of Australia edeposit 252635

Published by TIFFANY HOUSE AUSTRALIA

P.O BOX 532 CAMDEN 2570 NSW.

Foreword

For over forty years I have known Dave and I have always found him genuine and profoundly caring to those around him. Dave is direct and honest and has a rare ability to confront his pain and with rare insight, use it to build a better future for himself and his family. Dave and I have worked together, and he has become a very dear friend. I have seen God touch his life in many powerful ways.

Rev. Peter Thompson
Founding Pastor. Vision Church, Canberra.

Dave is a true Aussie larrikin with a plethora of stories that carry with them anecdotal lessons. With blatant honesty, he writes from a place of inspiration and wisdom. Today, he is as much of a detective as he was in this book, always exploring, researching, and investigating the importance of family and mateship (aka friendship).

Damien Tohr
Pastor Kings Church

Acknowledgments

My heartfelt thanks to Jenny Marsland, who has transformed my story into this book. I am eternally grateful for her tremendous support and skill.

To my wife, Kath, who persevered with me as I purposed to tell my story. We have been subject to life's most significant challenges, but God was faithful to sustain us no matter what. Thank you for staying the distance to see it through all these last fifty-nine years.

Thank you to all my associates, friends, and professionals who may or may not know the part they played in my development. Many of you have stood alongside me, encouraging me to run the race, fight the good fight and remain faithful to the One who saved me.

Without the presence of the Lord guiding me, I would have reverted to the ways of the world.

I feel so blessed to have been purchased with a price by Jesus Christ. Thank you, Dad, for bringing me to know who I am and whose I am!

Dave Poulton

Preface

I grew up in a time when people said whatever they wanted to say and as a result, kids were targeted with hurtful words. I could never be honest about my feelings, and cleverly concealed them by a well-constructed mask. To protect myself, I would climb my tree, my safe place. Then when my school years were over, I joined the Army as a regular soldier. The Vietnam War changed my personality from easy going to vindictive. I survived the war zone and climbed through the ranks in the Australian Federal Police to become the top in my field in bomb disposal…Twenty-two years there only added to my hidden distress with long hours away from home. Seventeen-hour days and many seven-day weeks were the norm. These long hours removed me from a father's role. Read how a sudden confrontation with my self-rejection and the revelation of the metaphoric trench in which I had lived, changed everything for me, including a wonderful change in my family life. Kath and I have three outstanding sons, but in their earlier years, I had become lost in my prodigal ways and had failed them as a father. At a point of total collapse, God stepped in and rescued me and my entire family from imminent ruin. Each of our sons have, with deep integrity, set their course in life and have stayed on track. Kath and I will celebrate our sixtieth wedding anniversary in 2024, and I look back amazed at the grace of my loving heavenly Father who accepted a lost prodigal. My wife has stood by me through incredible adversity and she still is my strength and guidance. I pray that the Holy Spirit will gently comfort those who need comforting and bring freedom to those who have been trapped by their self-beliefs, just as I had been trapped.

NOTE: This book might bring up things of the past, so please be kind to yourself!

The author of this book discusses themes relating to childhood trauma, and to the mental fallout occurring from war injuries. If this type of content is troubling or triggers memories from the past, please take care of yourself while reading.

Where to get help in Australia.

National Domestic, Family and Violence Counseling, a 24-hour information and support service for anyone in Australia. 1800respect.org.au or call 1800 737 732

Lifeline. 24/7 crisis support and suicide prevention services. Lifeline.org.au or call 131114-

Open Arms (Veteran and Family Counselling Service) In Australia 24 hr 1800011046

Introduction

The thing is, we blokes think it is childish of us to have emotional needs. "Seriously mate, just get on with it," we're told. But when the stomach ulcer appears, or we become a recluse, people look at us and think, "Surely, why can't he get the help he needs!" But how can we get help when we aren't supposed to have emotions?

When I was a kid living through the 1940 war years, emotions were at an all-time high and had to be suppressed afterward. I'd hear my Mum talk about traps and why loud noises kept everyone's nerves on edge. Other such stories screwed my image up and made me feel like I was the blame for certain things. If you were a child in the fifties, you might have felt you had stepped onto someone else's stage and were living out their life. This, for many a child, was the plight of being human.

My life probably was like yours if you had become lost in the matrix of life's disappointments and all the drama that brings. Were you allowed to cry and complain or show upset feelings? It was taboo in my day. When the Second World War ended, happiness danced on kitchen tables and in the streets, while those who lost loved ones hid their excruciating pain. Australia got back on its feet. Yet, all the while, the nation held tightly to its stoic ways including the idea that bravery calms painful emotions. But nothing could be further from the truth. The stiff upper lip and holding in emotional pain has since been found to be detrimental to our mental health.

Contents

Chapter 1	The Telegram	1
Chapter 2	The Boy	6
Chapter 3	The Tree	9
Chapter 4	My Pain Tank	15
Chapter 5	The Ticket	22
Chapter 6	Wedding Bells	27
Chapter 7	Flagging Ego	32
Chapter 8	Home	36
Chapter 9	Dad's Book	42
Chapter 10	Ambushed	49
Chapter 11	Adventures	55
Chapter 12	Awoken	61
Chapter 13	The Miracle	65
Chapter 14	Piercing Eyes	69
Chapter 15	Living The Dream	73
Chapter 16	The Mystery Meeting	77
Chapter 17	Ministry God's Way	80
Chapter 18	Heaven on Earth	86
Chapter 19	The Hug	89
Chapter 20	The Trench	93
Chapter 21	The Porch	99

You gave me wings to fly, then took away my sky [1]

PART ONE

Expectations can ruin our happiness

1
The Telegram

Blue skies and a soft breeze were typical when I was a kid. But not so much now, sixty years later, sudden gale-force and raging cyclonic winds blow out of nowhere. And more than ever, we have seen an increase in flooding. But it's the sizzling summers and out of control fire season we fear the most with its blistering oven-like winds. And that's what I felt when I opened the front door on that Saturday morning in January 2003. *Oh, that's a worry,* I thought as I tried pushing the door shut. None of us in Duffy had the slightest clue as to the impact that wind would have in creating its own firestorm.

Typically, a spark is all it takes, but these two fires had broken out many kilometers from home. High winds had fanned their flames into a 180-kilometer single fire front. Our hope the winds would redirect the fire away from Canberra were dashed on hearing news of it exploding in our pine forest! Chris, our eldest son, had kept a ten-day vigil on the fires, and just before lunch, on hearing the explosion, tore around to our place and found me just about to climb onto the roof. "Dad, what's going on?" He gasps. 'Quick, help me drench the gutters and plug the downpipes.' But it was too late. From the roof, I heard Kath yelling, "Chris get Dad off the top of the house." She kept screaming at us, but the thunderous roar of the firestorm drowned her piercing cry. 260-degree fireballs bounced from our side of the street to the other. Car tires melted on the disintegrating asphalt as high flames bore down upon the suburb. Neighbours fled—the fire truck didn't make it up the street, and houses around us collapsed into the furnace. In the middle of it all, the sky turned black. So black, neither Chris nor I knew what to do. Have you ever experienced that sort of sudden unknowing?

I have, and many times it had drawn hidden strength from within me. Like in Vietnam, when my mate whispered, "Don't move; a scorpion is poised to strike your forehead." The night bombings also had me, more than once, drawing inner strength to cope. But as a child, being told to take your worn-out jumper into your dark bedroom can be just as scary. A young mind employs imagination and a sense of wonder to pike up the courage.

As a ten-year-old, I'll tell you what happened and how the years growing up in Armidale shaped my earliest mindset.

In the dark I fumbled towards the wardrobe and opened it to a creaking of floorboards parting. My eyes were surprised to see a rather large shiny chest. Somehow, I knew my life would never make sense if that heavy lid remained shut. So I pried it open and saw in there everything Mum

Chapter 1 The Telegram

had kept hidden, including a secret that seemed to be in the early stages of its making. We will pick this up as we go along. But for now, the newest part of that secret had gotten my life off to a good start, with Mum waving a telegram in the air. "Daddy will be home soon," she said, twirling, looking her happiest. I don't know what *soon* means to you, but to a kid, *soon* means now. But the next day, through the following week, my siblings were poking their heads out the window expecting Dad to show up. After all, we were promised he'd come. Parents can promise in good faith things they only hope will happen. But be warned, kids remember!

My story concerns the impact Mum's secret had on me. After another year of living at our old address, we moved into a new commission house and ran around the rambling verandas and out onto the spacious backyard. We had a front fence, a blue letterbox and in the vacant block next door, a large pine tree. But at 81 Taylor Street, there was no dad. Mum was furious he had disappeared and had gone without giving a reason—he had just left. Whether Dad was muscly or thin, I cannot remember. But it still mattered; he hadn't seen me grow tall and wasn't aware of my fast legs winning last week's race. The more I stared at Dad's vacant chair at the dinner table, the emptier I felt!

I was six years old, and especially noticing his absence, I'd ask Mum, 'Where's Dad?' I expected Mum to answer me kindly, for gentleness was her usual way of relating with the neighbours. But shockingly, in an explosive fit, she turned to me and yelled, "I will spiflicate you if you ask that one more time!" I felt confused and angry, and kept asking, and Mum kept punishing me with her scary threats. I was so desperate to find my Dad I even took other brutal hits when Mum was in a bad mood. Nothing would stop my inquiring mind.

My older sister Deidre had very 'knowing' eyes and organised herself in beautiful finicky ways. Both my younger twin brothers were scallywags, and got themselves into mischief that I had to sort out. Even at their young age, Robert looked like the Poulton side of the family, and Raymond more like Mum's side. We'd be out in the backyard, kicking the soccer ball around, pretending life was perfectly fine. But knowing things were not okay, I'd think *someone must know why Dad isn't living with us.*

In the late afternoons, I stood on the front porch and as I watched the soft hues covering the western sky, I longingly hoped Dad would remember to come home. As the sun disappeared, my heart sank with it. In the mornings, I'd squint harder past the horizon hoping to see his face running towards me.

Most kids are much more emotionally aware than we think. Were you aware of your emotions, but did not tell anyone how you felt? I felt stuck—not that I knew what that meant, but on the football field one wintry weekend, the

Chapter 1 The Telegram

wild excitement on the sideline inspired me to "get moving in life." I caught the football and sprinted toward the goal posts. A bunch of my teammates caught up to me and pushed me along with their sweaty bodies until I fell over the try line. I lay there, hugging that leathery ball. As the roaring excitement eased and the long sound of the whistle faded, I heard, "You've done it! You have just won the game for your four-stone-seven-pound football team!" I sucked on the quarter orange, and thought, *if I can win a game for my team, maybe I could even find my Dad. If I could just see him, talk to him, tell him how much I want him, perhaps I could get him back.* On that hope, I fed my soul.

I felt hideously alone most of those early years, and I mean, really alone. It was painful. Nonetheless, life continued on and the cricket game went ahead at school in the springtime despite the freezing northerly winds blowing around us. In reply to the teacher's insistence, I looked at the oversized gloves and thought, *seriously, there must be one brave soul amongst us.* I called out, 'I will try them.' Though way too big, I caught the ball and was about to stump the batter when his bat hit my face. I fell, screaming, fully expecting to die. I felt gutted that I had no dad to fetch me or help me tolerate the pain of a broken nose. Recuperating was dreadful, and life generally was excruciating.

2
The Boy

Were you ever stubborn? I was. I didn't like school after that cricket episode and didn't want to be there. I'd get off the early morning bus and head down to the creek where I enjoyed the sound of my own thoughts as I played in the water. But finding solace in doing my own thing abruptly ended at the sight of my Uncle Ross who scowled, "I've been sent to find you." I have faint memories of a loud voice towering over me, a flogging, then being picked up by the scruff of my neck and marched home. Mum typically, was waiting to frighten me with another flogging if I did that again.

> The hardest thing you'll ever do is to comfort a crying child when their father doesn't come to see them. [2]

Mum had horrendous challenges to overcome and many saw her as a formidable woman. She was a battler and to feed and clothe us, worked three jobs. On Saturdays, Mum went out and left us, the boys, at home. Before she did, she stuck a "to-do" list on the fridge and then called out, "No mischief today!" Of course, Mum had often come home to a drama of some sort. While my older sister Deidre, organised

Chapter 2 - The Boy

herself to go out with friends, I turned to my twin brothers and winked. We had hours, sometimes an entire day, to find all sorts of mischief to get up to. The twins, though inseparable, got on each other's nerves. One morning, we boys were bored and at a loose end. In self-defense against what Raymond had already done to him, Bobby grabbed the peeling knife and let it fly. The blade narrowly missed my hip, 'You're in for it now!' I yelled. With that, another knife came whizzing past my knee, hitting the door. And sure enough, when Mum got home and saw the blades in the sink, she flew into a rage.

Pop Poulton lived two blocks away. He rarely was upset, and happily gave me a taste of soul connection with his friendly chats. He was my ally and favourite Grandpa, a jolly old fellow, always had me laughing as we played Two-Up. Yet, at times his eyes looked sad, and I often wondered what he was thinking.

Uncle John's eyes sparkled like the sun on the water and his big grin was the size of his beautiful heart. Our Sunday lunches gave me a chance to ask him about Dad's whereabouts. After some pestering, he eventually said something about him being in Batlow, "That's all I'm telling you!" It was all the information I needed. *Batlow*, I wondered, *where on earth is that? Reckon it isn't far from here?*

The Boy the Tree and the Trench

Being abandoned or given up is the most devastating emotion.[3]

There was a lot of drama at our place, but the family picnics were a welcomed respite. We thrived on fairy bread and a lot of boisterousness. I thought a lot about my Dad at those picnics and often imagined him there with us.

Our two large front windows were hard to lock and Mum, with her vivid imagination, feared intruders might climb in. So as to hear their footprints, she'd stay awake all night, knitting us jumpers and catch up on sleep during the day. In the holidays, we had to keep the house extra quiet—so quiet, I could hear Mum whispering to her friends, "My days at the convent were worse than this!" Uncle Ross knew more than he let on and I could tell that by his particular focus in life. In a forlorn sort of a way, he kept reiterating, drumming into us about this "hard, cruel world."

Hmm, cruel, I thought. At church, the hard seats were a punishment in themselves, and the constant bells distressed me. The Latin was enough already, so I'd excuse myself to the bathroom during the catechism classes and loiter in the park nearby. Only to race back to catch the last bit of the story about an angry, cruel God who didn't like children. I'd always come home from that church feeling like I had lost something very important.

3
The Tree

Did you have enough fun when you were a kid? I wanted to be happy *all* of the time. Yet, at home I got the impression life was going to be tough, no matter what! Rather than feeling sorry for myself, I had all the fun I needed conjuring up pranks and other push-backs.

"I can hear your Mum yelling at you kids," Mrs. Jones from across the road said, and then worriedly confronted me with, "Are you all OK over there?" To answer her question, when I saw her children coming up the street and, in a larrikin mood, I jumped out from behind my hedged fence with a "Boo; my mother will spiflicate you!" They screamed and their frightened feet bolted across the road calling out to their mother. *Well,* I thought, *that's what I have to put up with.*

I didn't know the word spiflicate meant destruction. But my gut knew it! And so did the milkman's instinct. He took off when I pranked him with a mere mention of the word. Mum saw him running up the street and me dashing down the side of the house, and knowing I was the culprit, chased me. But I had already jumped over the fence and had shimmied up my pine tree. I was pretty high up, and that made it extra fun. As I aimed pinecones at specific targets below, I could hear Mum angrily calling me, "Get down now, you can't stay there all day!" Mum could never break my spirit. No matter how hard she tried, even with all the gut-wrenching floggings, she could never tame me. Mum still had a bunch of fun-loving kids on her hands. Kids are naturally fun-loving and fun became my "go-to" place.

On Saturdays, we were home alone, and out came the white socks. We'd slip and slide from the lounge room into the kitchen on the shiny lino. Then, a mighty crash as Bobby's head slammed into the glass cabinet. Hours later, Mum walked into a deadly silent house and thought, *I will put the kettle on and make a cup of tea and find those boys; they might be next door.* Through into the kitchen, she hopped over the shattered glass. Furiously, her short legs tore out through the back door and at the top of her voice, called, "David!! Raymond!!! Get down from that tree now!" Bobby was under his bed, waiting for the uproar, and at the sound of Mum's feet, poked his sore head out, dusting off comics in his hand. You guessed it - we each copped it that afternoon.

A tiny woman, and to pull us into line, Mum created the scariest looks on her face, and turned herself into a giant with that big stick in hand. Kids must be safe when a giant lives in the house, but I wasn't safe. I screamed, 'Help, get me out of here!' Mum shouted, "If you don't stop crying, I'll give you something to cry about!"

Chapter 3 - The Tree

Frustrated and frightened, I felt gutted that even my tears were punishable.

> I cannot think of any need in childhood
> as strong as his need for a father's protection.
> Sigmund Freud. (Bhatt, 2020) [4].

Being the oldest boy, I had to walk Mum to the Court House every second Thursday. Even there, I felt Mum's stern instructions, "Walk on the other side of me, near the gutter; that way, you'll protect me from the traffic." Being the larrikin that I was, I tried making that an adventure - at least fun! But instead, the effort of walking with my feet turned out was enough already, and to arrive and be told, "Sorry, Ma'am, no money from Mr. Poulton today," was even more discouraging. But Mum, holding a hand-out of a twenty-pound note to see the family through, stood forlornly on the footpath, and with it, her hurtful rhetoric about men. This is where it all began affecting me.

Her words were scary, but it was her tone that frightened me. It wasn't so much *what* Mum said; it was the *way* she said it that gave me the biggest stomach aches. Even though I was a brave sort of a kid, I still ran at the site of danger. But as dangerous as Mum's tone sounded, I didn't run. Instead, I froze on the spot and pretended her words didn't bother me.

> Abandonment issues stem from the belief
> that someone leaving was your fault.
> Shandel Stewart. [5]

The Boy the Tree and the Trench

I pretended my life was fine and that it was OK that I had no father at home to ruffle my hair at breakfast or take me away on weekend adventures. Pretending became my norm. Even when I failed an exam, or had to face other hideous situations alone I pretended to be absolutely fine.

> When a child can't calm down,
> they need connection and comfort,
> not criticism and control. Jane Evans.[6]

As an eighteen-year-old, I'll reflect on some of my experiences that made my teenage years even tougher to bear.

Have you felt abandoned with no chance of ever being found? By the end of primary school, I felt so lost and very alone. Life had become even scarier as high school, and all its unknowns, loomed large in my mind. Still, walking into an empty house with no dad, all I ever wanted was some tender care from Mum. None of us boys at home got any hugs or goodnight kisses—no pats on the back or other such tenderness. I dreamt about having warm, caring arms to hold me and helpful words to encourage me. I needed someone to help calm my anxious thoughts and make me feel I belonged on this earth.

> When little people are overwhelmed
> by big emotions, it is our job to share our calm,
> not join their chaos. L.R Knost. [7]

Chapter 3 - The Tree

Dierdre was spoken to gently, and was called sweet pea and honey-bun, and in no way told to suck it up princess. In our culture, girls were helpless dames, and as the story goes, we boys, their knights dressed in shining armour, ready to fight off dragons with our invincible powers. I thought it unfair that cultural rhetoric followed the idea that boys were stoic and brave, with no need to talk about their emotions. But with the drama of a dad missing, I had plenty of out-of-control emotions to talk about!

Perhaps you have skidded off your bike and were called names when caught crying? Our nervous system releases an emotional response to danger the same way as the female's nervous system does. So, we boys should cry when we feel pain and should be given some tender care when our hearts are broken. Yet how many times did I hear Mum in the kitchen, "Oh, boys don't need sentimental soppiness. It will turn them into girls. And mind you, Mable," she said to our neighbour, "Bringing a boy up with that sort of weakness is seriously forbidden." These sorts of old-wives-tales are a crime to our gender and have created a culture whereby men silently suffer.

Though Pop Poulton kept everything to himself—he didn't let me suffer in silence. At a Sunday lunch, he saw me crying and put his arm around me and asked me about my sadness. If anything his gentle approach gave me strength. Despite the cultural rhetoric, we males have a soft side and should talk about things that worry or cause us grief. How many of us are holding in pain just for appearances sake? Me and my brothers did a lot of that—for to cry would have shown a weakness in us. Mind you, I never saw Mum cry. She personally viewed emotions as dangerous. Mum's biggest nightmare was her fear we'd crumble under life's weight and she would not be able to put us back together again. At the very least, I hoped a simple hug might help me feel seen and heard. According to Mum though, being held in her arms was rather needless, and way too risky, she couldn't cope with us chancing some kindness from her.

It was Mum's new puppy that saved us from our need to tiptoe around the house. She was the happy topic of most conversations. I just wanted to be loved like Flo. Her little watchdog ears would have her race to the door at full speed. "She's happy to see you," Mum told the visitors. I wanted to be noticed in that way. With Flo, Mum was always in a good mood. She'd put on her sweetest voice, "You're such a gorgeous little puppy, here, have some brekky." Even when Flo tore up Mum's *New Idea*, she was never yelled at. *The spoilt brat!* If anything, we boys just wanted to be spoken to properly, and Mum had no idea that, amid all of this, a horrid feeling of being unloved grew within me.

4
My Pain Tank

Armidale was a hidden diamond as far as country towns go. All heart is how I'd describe the people. When the sun warmed the streets, everyone emerged with the jams made during the winter months. Stalls, music, and festivities were a normal part of life once the snow had melted.

At 81 Taylor Street, I'd always be in strife. One afternoon, to escape another drama, I fled on my bike and rode up the main street as fast as possible. Hurrying past the local pub, I had turned into the alleyway when my eye caught sight of a wad of twenty-pound notes on the ground. I skidded to a halt. Judging by its weight, suddenly, I was the richest kid in town. *No one would miss a single twenty-pound note in a wad that big*, so I stuffed one into my handlebar and rode off to the police station. After answering some questions and being patted on the back, I called, 'Bye, I am off to the Pictures now.'

Mum had lots of support to manage us kids - such as Uncle Blue and Aunt Biddy, the neighbours, plus the other Poultons living in town. And, of course, Cyril. He was the local Police Sergeant and promised Mum he'd keep me out of harm's way. He was like a dad to me, personally coming to the cinema to fetch me after the owner reported his money lost. Cyril took me to the police station where the missing cash was returned and, in his stern Sergeant's voice, said, "I hope this is the last time I have to keep you from trouble, Davey." I just nodded, hopped on my bike, and skedaddled home.

I had been peddling into the driveway when I rode smack-bang into trouble again. Cyril was at the front door telling Mum everything. "I will give you one thing, Joan," he said, "David is resourceful. He meant well; I am asking you to go easy on him; he's already had a big scolding."

"Sure," she sighed as Cyril walked off down the path. But with a fire I hadn't seen in a long time, Mum eyeballed me. It was after that flogging I outrightly blamed my Dad. I was overwhelmed. I needed to get that painful judgement stashed out of sight, so I created my own special Pain Tank inside my heart. Whenever upset, I'd emit squirts of rage, and sad smoke trailed behind me.

> Feelings are valid,
> and you have every right to feel
> whatever emotion
> you want. You are not being dramatic,
> nor are you
> exaggerating. [8]

Stashing rage into my Pain Tank made life even more miserable for me. Within our Taylor Street house, I felt trapped. I was too young to run away. So, on my twelfth birthday, I decided when old enough to leave home, I'd pack

Chapter 4 - My Pain Tank

my bags, forget about ever finding Dad, and never return! Yet, escaping those painful stories would not be easy and became a lifelong endeavour.

> When you grow up
> with an absent father,
> you grow up way too fast. [9]

"Don't worry, Mrs. Poulton. It takes a village to raise kids these days," said the neighbour who lived two doors up from Mrs. Jones. That gave me hope, for if ever there was a kid who was unloved and not wanted, it was me. Cyril understood my stories, knew about my pain and was my safe place and as such, I made him a pivotal part of my village. He kept a close eye on me, and watched out for my good friends, the Fletcher brothers. They weren't in the same classes at school as me, but none-the-less lived close by on a high hill in a run-down house with their mother. They were also searching for their dad.

Even in the summer, they, like me, had cold icy feelings covering their soul. Only when Cyril saw us roaming the streets, did some of that coldness disappear. "Hop in boys," he said as if happy to see us. Into his wagon we jumped to be driven home to our mothers. But then, more optimistic than usual, he said, "I have signed you all up for the Police Boys Club; it's brand new." Cyril's team of kindhearted men rallied around us boys and created that club to be a safe place, a home, a place to solve problems and be caught

The Boy the Tree and the Trench

up in something bigger than ourselves. By the time I had my fifteenth birthday, my village had given me a sense of belonging. I happily signed up for the Army Cadets and began training for a life of service. Also, I played the drums in our School Cadet Band and became the Drum Major, leading in various marches and street parades.

The winter months were predictable and I would watch them transmute through into spring and then into my favourite, the blistering summer months. Another year had passed, and the town was bursting with colour. With the sun warming my back, I'd peddle my bike up the narrow streets, take my feet off the pedals, and glide down the steep decline. The long days, riding my bike around town, soaking up the summer heat, were the best days of the year.

Fun helps kids forget their troubles, and boys especially love a bit of fun. On weekends, the Fletcher boys and I would be out of town on our bikes, riding through the scrub, searching for the best swimming spots and waterfalls. We three dug deep within ourselves to find the courage necessary to live a fatherless life. To prove we could do whatever we wanted, we hid in the stormwater channel on the outskirts of Armidale. Whenever a semi-trailer slowed down to turn the corner, we'd jump on, and the driver would unknowingly have three teenagers holding on to the back as it crawled up the hill. We would then jump off at Benvenu Primary School. One night in the darkness, though, we didn't see

Chapter 4 My Pain Tank

the primary school, and we spent the next twenty-five miles riding in sheer terror. At the next town, we jumped off and hiked it home.

I loved the thrill of these adventures but when I got home Mum came out swinging her stick. With a look of terror on her face, she screamed, "It's after midnight, everybody's out looking for you!" I was starving and tried explaining about the semi-trailer episode. But none of that mattered and instead I was given a fair beating. Hot tears saturated my lumpy pillow. I sobbed, not because of the welts across the back of my legs but because I was all alone. I had no love in my heart for anyone. I hated Mum. I hated Armidale. I hated Cyril. Angry and hurt, I felt sad and without hope of ever finding someone who'd care about things that mattered to me.

I had created my own village but I needed someone under the same roof as me. Foster parents would love me and give me a lot of attention. Indeed, they wouldn't throw me out into a hot desert to be scorched by life as it appeared my next-door neighbours had been. During the school holidays, they'd call in at our place for a cup of tea. Mum would humour them with a tea-leaf reading, but I saw fear in their eyes as they paced back and forth. To catch the gossip, I'd stand behind the wall and listen to their whisperings. "The skeletons come out eventually," my Uncle Blue told me while crunching on a granny smith apple with him in the backyard one day. And they did. When I opened Mum's golden chest, I discovered Pop was also abandoned when he was a kid. And my Uncle Blue had some stuff I couldn't understand or make sense of, so it is no use trying to explain what I saw there.

I also had a secret —a doozy of a one, the absolute bane of my life. I always knew I'd never get to know my dad or even find him. And I sensed I was the blame —which, long ago, had thrown me into a survival mindset. I saw myself as a survivor, but not the sort of kid who'd wallow or who'd feel sorry for himself, for that was a waste of time. It was also useless telling Bill about my troubles—for what would my best mate know about family war-zones anyway? Rather, to get rid of that shame of being blamed, I decided I'd rise from my ashes and reinvent myself. I'd become invincible, fill my walls with accolades and become more of a boy than already am now, nothing would faze me, dampen my mood or influence the way I saw myself. I would know who I was and, one day, know Whose I was.

My pushbike and I were inseparable. We went everywhere together, and it even got me a job as a paperboy. Peddling around the neighbourhood late afternoons gave me the very power for which I had been searching. I felt good that I could earn my own money and be more in control of my fragile life. As the newspapers bounced and my whistle blew, I thought, *I might even be a policeman one day; then*

Chapter 4 - My Pain Tank

I would let everyone know who's boss.

I was sad about many things, but especially sad to see the end of summer. The days were even colder at the end of autumn, and nights fell quickly. One particular winter, my bike light kept dimming, and to brighten it, I pushed on the dynamo with my outstretched leg. It didn't work, and frustrated, I pushed so hard the wheel buckled. I was flung off my seat, over the handlebars and landed on the sharp edge of the gutter. "Ouch!" With a sore back and a spinning head, I picked myself up, threw the crumpled mess over my shoulder, and walked three and a half miles home in the dark. The dark never frightened me. Yet, during a full moon, I felt an uneasy disquiet disturbing my soul. I looked upon the slumbering world around me and mused upon my decision. I would become everything I ever wanted to become and prove to the world I could make it on my own.

5
The Ticket

Mum was her happiest when pulling out weeds in the garden and planting daffodil and jonquil bulbs in the winter. But what goes on outside in the yard can be altogether different to what goes on inside. Behind closed doors, our house felt more like a continual storm and I remember back to one of those years. I had achieved a lot, yet I had become stuck inside Mum's tangled image of me.

To cheer myself and fill that ever-deepening emptiness, I became the classroom larrikin. Instead of focusing on Shakespeare and other complex subjects in Year Nine, I'd have a group of boys laughing at my jokes at the back of the classroom. When I had gotten everyone distracted and the teacher had enough, I was sent to the principal's office. The cane stung, but that very long walk home after detention hurt the most.

It was tough being a brainy kid who got himself into all sorts of mischief. It was with half a smile on his face when my science teacher was summonsed to the quadrangle to settle the near miss I had with my explosives. He boomed, "Where did you get them from?" But it was my Physical Ed teacher who gave me my biggest chance at success. He sent me to various state carnivals and bragged about the

Chapter 5 - The Ticket

track and field records I had set there. During his classes, he said, "Your natural athletic talent is extraordinary. Apply yourself, work hard, and never give up." With that sort of encouragement, nothing could stop me.

With my focus on athletics, I fell behind academically in Year Twelve, but I saw the invitation to repeat the year as opportunity to increase my star athletic performance in javelin, the long triple jump, and some track events. I barely studied– in fact, studying was almost non-existent. Rather, I spent my time coaching a women's basketball team full of pretty faces and agile bodies. During practice days, Mum thought I was at a mate's place studying from a maths book.

Months later, after hearing a mighty scream, I ran inside the house to find Mum sitting in her armchair, waving the Armidale Express around wildly, unmanneredly holding up my photo as the coach of that basketball team. 'That's right, Mum, I trained those girls, and now they're champions!' I glanced down at those winners. More so, I smiled mainly because I had become proficient at organising my life the way I wanted. A fortnight later, I returned from a referee camp in Sydney to rumours the Poulton lad was the best.

One girl especially caught my eye. She liked my fairness on the court, and I liked her long curly hair and dreamt about us being together. At the formal dance, we snuck off in the middle of my favourite song. The air was fresh, and the night sky exceptionally starry. We found a

The Boy the Tree and the Trench

quiet spot on one of the classroom verandas, and under the stars, we were chatting when I threw my arms around her, and we held each other tightly. I kissed her; it was a special moment. But not even her warm personality could entice me to stay. I had already signed up for the army and was keener than ever on leaving that town.

Early January 1962, my ticket out of Armidale came in our blue letterbox. I was on my way to Wagga with other army recruits to undertake a ten-week training course. The day I was ready to leave, I stood before Mum hoping to hug her. Clearly she had not changed her tune, for I could not even get her to smile. No doubt it was because I had joined the army that she looked worried and sternly said, "You will turn out to be like your father!" It was a painful moment, but I left town with that poisoned arrow piercing my heart. I was finished with my home life and all that it didn't have to offer.

On the platform, getting a smile from either Raymond or Robert was near impossible. My brothers just stood there with teary eyes and waved as the train began moving. I mused; *I will miss those tigers for sure*. Even so, at the sound of the heavy engine puffing smoke, I was glad to leave Armidale. To celebrate, my best mate offered me a muffin. Always smiling, not much bothered Bill. Little wonder, both parents were seen waving him off. Other dads were on the platform too. Shortly after we got going, Bill

Chapter 5 - The Ticket

joined a little crowd further back and left me alone with my thoughts. I folded my arms tightly and thought back to how Mum's angry outbursts had crushed my spirit. When feeling especially stuck, I'd tell myself, *just comply; otherwise, you might get spiflicated and be blown up into a million pieces.*

I was in an unhappy mood. *Perhaps if I had a dad, the weights would be lighter. But they aren't, and I need someone to help me carry them; I am unloved – and another hefty weight - I don't belong- I am nothing but a pest at home, and 'that boy' from Taylor Street.* Always before, but more so now, I felt like a little lost child searching for his dad. Deep from within, I called out, *Dad, where are you? I am hurting, and I want you.* I was furious I'd have to strive for that elusive self-acceptance. It scared me to think. What if the search never ends?

At Kapooka, the home of the 1st Recruit Training Battalion, I strolled into the barracks. I looked around, tossed my bag onto my bed, and found the mess hall. With relief, I mused - *at least I had escaped the frying pan at home.* Little did I know I was about to be thrown into the fire.

PART TWO

*The army was more than a job.
It was my leverage to fame.*

6
Wedding Bells

My need for love took me to the brink of disaster. I have been retired now for several years and tell the rest of this story sitting in my study, overlooking a lush garden.

The Platoon Officers at Wagga seemed to have forgotten a few things, like how to smile and be kind when speaking. When around them, I felt sucked into a firestorm. When two blazing eyes and a mouth full of fire came screaming at me, I held my breath for fear I'd swallow his fumes.

"P o u l t o n!! I thought, *hang on, sweetheart, not so fast.* Barely drawing breath, he yelled, "You are so low on the human scale you could crawl under a snake with an umbrella up!"

"P o u l t o n!! If your brain were explosives, you wouldn't have enough to blow a matchbox apart!"

"What the…" said Bill as we walked away from that first drill session.

'Yeah, his tone was loaded! I've had a gut full.' I tried pulling myself together as we walked off that unit parade ground. Later that afternoon, I was still fuming. I had put up with a lot from Mum and thought I was above the pain of it all. But while Mum could not break my spirit, I thought *this sort of aggressive energy can destroy a bloke*. Typically, this went underground in me and my mates and I brushed off his ranting with a good laugh. Along with Bill and the others, I decided to enjoy the food at the mess hall, make the most of our training and finish the course with top marks.

After ten grueling weeks, my mates and I were on the bus, waiting to leave. We were laughing and jostling around when out of nowhere, our platoon sergeant popped his head inside the door. *Oh, here's trouble*, I thought. He looked up and down at us and said, "All you who are going to Infantry, I will see you at home; the rest of you, forget I ever knew you!" His poisoned arrow pierced my heart. That sergeant was our first casualty in Vietnam. Some of us on that bus got together and partied hard—such was his effect on us.

I had become a devoted corporal with a clean record, and it was suggested I'd make an excellent lieutenant, so I applied for Duntroon. Yet, that application didn't meet the criteria, and at the daytime interview, I was refused entry. I was utterly devastated. Honestly, with the rhetoric spewed at me in Wagga and the emotional pain I had grown up with - what hope did I have? My childhood weights were still sitting heavily upon me. *The Poulton clan are the problem, and now I am tangled up in all of their pain. My true*

Chapter 6 - Wedding Bells

buoyant, fun-loving self had gone missing in action. I put all that behind me, and thrived on power and control. With organizational and leadership skills beyond my age, the Commanding Officer watched me complete tasks within impressive time frames. In my final unit, I became a Field Engineer Troop Sergeant—the youngest ever. I could not have been happier, so much so, I began looking for a social life. My mate, who had grown up in the area, suggested I find that meeting where lots of young people were hanging out together on weekends.

Liverpool's public transport made it easy to get around. I popped into a fish and chip shop opposite the railway station for a Coke. A few girls were loitering in there, but it was the tall, slim girl who caught my eye. I asked her about the meeting, and as it turned out, they had just bought dinner before going there themselves. I smiled and said to her, 'I'll come with youse.' To that, she said, "You are not my type, I am not interested in men in uniform." But her sparkling eyes and gorgeous smile said something altogether different. Kath told me later she had fallen in love with my strikingly handsome face, and I told her of my hard job at making her *no* a *yes*.

That night, Kath introduced me to everyone at the Catholic youth group, and I was welcomed with open arms. The blokes invited me to join their basketball practice after work on Wednesdays and I went onto become a valued team member. Any excuse is a good excuse to get out of the city and on a summer's weekend, a bus trip to Warragamba Dam with the group sealed a new fate for me. During an outdoor game, Kath and I were in a feisty battle to win but that ended when I over leapt my jump and sprained my ankle. Kath graciously offered me her shoulder while I limped back to the bus and we began dating. I enjoyed her veracious personality and my affection for her had me catching buses in and out of Liverpool four times a week, twice on weekends. She was the oldest of nine children, and like me, also had an unhappy family life.

In a precious moment on a wintry night in 1963, while kissing Kath goodnight on her back steps, I proposed to my sweetheart. The following January, vows were made and to the sound of pealing church bells, Kath and I walked out into a glaringly sunny forty-one-degree afternoon.

My Nana, dad's mother, was notorious for causing a stir and hassling over photo shoots at wedding receptions. But we survived her rant, and made happier memories on the dance floor. Then I enjoyed a week of bleached beaches and moonlit dinners honeymooning with the girl of my dreams. My army life seemed a distant memory but after a blissful entry into married life, I quickly returned to the School of Military Engineering. A few months later, I received the happy news that in less than a year, Kath and I would welcome a gorgeous little boy into our family.

Chapter 6 - Wedding Bells

In the meantime I had gained top marks in the Demolition Supervisor's Course. Twelve months later I was transferred to Wagga as a Corporal Drill Instructor and Kath and Christopher came with me. While there, Darren was born in the October. A few months later I had been promoted to Sergeant and Kath and my boys and I were transferred to Holsworthy.

In order to survive the heart-stopping assault courses during the two-and-a-half months of jungle warfare training I had pushed myself beyond anything I had ever known. It was every bit of hell defying death in a matrix of ambush drills and, plying my way through jungle terrain in abject darkness on night patrols. Yet this training had shown me, though spent and pushed beyond all limits, I had it within me to conquer all and every obstacle.

This was my final preparation for combat, but was it enough? No! It seemed not. I was devastated at news filtering through that our engineers in Vietnam were being killed in action. It rocked me to the core some working on tunnel clearance tasks had also been killed. I felt pushed to the edge, for Vietnam was my next stop. I was twenty-four years old, and the grief of dying an early death was unbearable. If I died, my two boys would not have a father at home to ruffle their hair at breakfast and take them on weekend adventures — or hear about their troubles.

7
Flagging Ego

A handful of mates, my bewildering heart, and a sick stomach boarded the RAAF Hercules. During the thunderous roar at takeoff, I hoped we'd fly over the Harbour side, to farewell the city and get a final glimpse of a world I had known and loved. But disappointedly, from Richmond Air base, we flew straight out towards the Simpson Desert. I tried adjusting my ears to the deafening drone and pondered what might lay ahead—then, took a deep breath and thought, *I hope we all make it home alive.* Bravely, I closed my eyes and slipped into a tenuous moment thinking about my two little boys.

Hours later we arrived in Vietnam and stepped out into a tropical land ravished by war. As a Troop Sergeant posted to the 17 Construction Squadron, I had instructions to take a contingent of sappers to Nui Dat in support of units as needed. Adjusting to the sites and smells at Nui Dat took time. I knew explosives would be part of my everyday life, but nothing could prepare me for the horrifying breadth of it all. One sweltry afternoon, some of us were bumping along on a dirt road in the back of a canvas-drawn army truck. Suddenly, a mighty explosion threw us all onto the truck's floor, and my nerves exploded with it. The other artillery

Chapter 7 - Flagging Ego

fire missions reminded us of the seriousness of our presence there. I had come to Vietnam knowing who I was and where I was going in life and in many ways, I had a strong internal compass. Yet a war zone can significantly damage your sense of direction, and in those early days, I could feel the tight grip I had on my life loosening. As such, I could not imagine having a future beyond Vietnam.

The sixty-two personnel in our contingent set up camp and built pits near their tents. The trench was my safe place. I had a few good mates, and their cheerful comradeship and moral support gave me a level of acceptance I had barely known possible. In a bid to stay calm, I had a choice, either to "worry myself sick" or spend my free time drinking and getting drunk. I hid my fear in a gurgling glass of ale. Cheap as dirt, beer was around ten cents, and cigarettes went for nothing. Even a forty-ounce bottle of whiskey was only two dollars. Drowning my sorrows in beer and whisky was the kindest thing I could do for myself.

All the while, back in Sydney, Kath, not knowing whether I was dead or alive, had taken herself to the brink of worry. She agonised over receiving a visit from the army and the padre with the dreaded news that I had been killed or severely maimed in Vietnam. Over morning tea, she and her friends sat around kitchen tables listening to the radio and heard of family members killed in action. At night Kath couldn't sleep. She'd be up at 2 am, washing floors and hanging clothes on the line, pacing back and forth, drinking coffee, and praying that God would keep me safe. How many times did she pray that prayer? She reckons thousands. Stuck in a whirlwind of terror, Kath quickly became a nervous wreck. But her worry was never mentioned in her letters. She kept them brief in the same way I had kept my letters to her brief. I was heartbroken and numbed my pain with whisky. In situations too hard to bear, it said, "Don't go back home, for you will be out of your depth, don't go there."

But I did go home for a brief leave—and happily gave my two little boys a huge daddy hug. Yet the ten days were spent battling a ruined gut, unable to eat all the deliciousness Kath served. I dubbed myself an angry so-and-so. But Kath saw beyond the anger. She had fallen in love with my kind and caring nature long ago and wanted the old me back home with her. To hold each other safe within each other's arms. Kath kept her grief from our little sons and gave them a sense of normality. Her deep faith in God and compassionate motherly ways prevented Chris and Darren from suffering a cold, dismissive home life.

I tried to make each day count with my family. Yet the days had become long and drawn out, and in no time, the whistling kettle reminded me of being spiflicated. In my son's tears, I'd see my childhood terror. I tried to avoid the memories, but in the corridors of my mind, they came

Chapter 7 - Flagging Ego

crashing down upon me—in one big jumbled, disorganised mess. Haunted by it all, I fell into a fearful belief that I would become an absent dad just as my father had been absent. This affected my confidence in a way I would never have imagined.

Kath had no idea about the stories in my head or the arrows my heart had taken–I needed someone to understand my invisible wounds. Finally, I found a cap that knew exactly what I was going through. It read, "Not all wounds are visible," and after I bought it, no one could get it off my head. One day, frustrated with me and out of sorts with herself, Kath said, "I married you, not the bloody army!"

After ten sunny, heart wrenching days, I was on my way back to Vietnam. At the airport, Kath and I bravely smiled at each other, yet, underneath my smile, I knew I could not articulate my pain or the fear I'd lose my way in life. As we said our goodbyes, I hugged Kath tighter than usual and lingered over a short kiss.

I then turned towards the door and about to walk through into the International Terminal when I heard Christopher crying out for his Daddy. I turned to see him running after me. Typically he was aware of everything happening around him— just like I had been when I was a child. In one of her letters, Kath told me my little boy thought a lot about me and wanted his daddy home to read him stories and play outside with him.

8
Home

At Nui Dat the long explosive night operations were exponentially terrifying but becoming dead to my little boys was the most terrifying of all. I'd wake to a new day as if it was my last—though I was grateful for the trench as it was my best chance at staying alive, yet, even there, anything could happen. The night, however, I had crawled into my sleeping bag I was too tired to worry about unknowns. When my feet couldn't reach the end of my sleeping bag, I thought my troops had short-sheeted me, but whatever it was moved violently, and terrified, I jumped out of my bag, grabbed my machete, and hacked the cobra *and* my sleeping bag to pieces.

In the dead of another night, my mate's whisper was full of dire urgency, "Sarge, don't move, don't even blink; a scorpion is perched on your shoulder, ready to strike your temple!" My terror was typical, yet it was expected I'd brush it off as if it meant nothing. I had been used to pretending nothing mattered, and especially threw all caution to the wind at the Eifel bridging course. After being sent there, I just did not care. There wasn't much to learn, and to fill in the time, the larrikin in me suggested my corporal mate and I take a joy flight to an American base for the day. We

Chapter 8 - Home

were flown in by helicopter. Wearing our Aussie slouch hats and greens, the corporal and I strolled into the barracks. It was chaos; some Americans were intoxicated, so we joined them in their drunkenness.

It was here I did crazy things in stupid situations. We got so inebriated that we missed our flight and had to wait two days before returning. To punish my larrikin ways, I was summoned to court. While waiting, they got me busily working on land clearing operations at the foot of the Long Hills south of Dat Do. While there, I was medevacked to Vung Tau 1 Field Hospital in excruciating pain. The Catholic priest didn't care about my battle wounds. He was more interested in getting a confession from me–I didn't believe in God, so I gave him a firm no and a see you later from me. At the court hearing, I lost my Sergeant ranking. I was suspended from duties for nineteen days, just long enough to recuperate, and, having decided to get out of the army, enjoy my final days in Vietnam, boozing to pass the time.

I had enough and wanted out. When I called it quits, my Troop Commanding Officer was not happy and said, "You know, I am losing one of my best men if you resign." A week later, on the verge of signing my resignation, he severely criticised me for being a turncoat. He allowed me to reconsider, insisting I withdraw my resignation. I refused, and with further threats, he told me to get out of his office.

The Boy the Tree and the Trench

Both he and I had issues, and we were at loggerheads trying to assert power over each other—the demoted Sergeant versus the Major. The next thing I knew, I had been called back into his office. "Your time is up." Then begrudgingly he sighed and said, "Pack up your gear, get all the necessary unit clearances, and be at the Kangaroo Pad by 1400 hours."

Roaring touchdowns were a big part of my life, but this one was different. I was home to stay. I gathered my gear, stumbled through quarantine, and stepped into the subzero night air. I thumbed a lift, and the familiar Aussie accent said, "Hop in, so where are you off to, mate?"

'To Holsworthy, I am just in from Vietnam,' I gasped. "Oh, welcome back legend, I bet you're glad to be home!"

"Who is rattling my window," thought Kath jumping from her bed. Though nervy, she never imagined it'd be me. But on pulling back the blinds, she discovered dreams do come true—her army husband standing there dressed in his summer clobber, smiling at her. The next day, at the army office, I was told, "You have two weeks to vacate the premises, or the Liverpool Sheriff will forcibly remove you." *Welcome home digger*! We continued our battle on that political front, and I replied, 'They can try. But I will put up a stormy fight.' He laughed and taunted me with, "They will use extreme force." Disheartened the government I faithfully had served had cast me aside, my anger gauge broke. When I handed Kath the eviction notice,

Chapter 8 Home

she rang a local newspaper, and went to war with the entire story. The next day, thousands of copies were thrown onto suburbia's front lawns and Sydneysiders read the headlines, "Army Stays Eviction." The eviction threats were scrapped for three months–enough to purchase a house in Maryvale, Western Sydney, for 21,500 dollars. With that out of the way, I now had to look for work. It wasn't easy, for no one wanted to employ a Vietnam Vet and I took this to mean I was worthless and no one cared about me.

The drinking culture in Vietnam had drastically changed my persona and greatly impacted how I lived out my days there. Now at home my mates and I spent a lot of time in the local pubs. When Kath kissed me goodbye just before lunch, I knew she'd be happy to see me again in a few short hours. But by the time I came home that evening, she avoided my eyes. It seemed she knew those hours were spent with my buddies, singing our pain away. After dinner, I saw vacant eyes staring back at me in the bathroom mirror. It was shocking that I felt so lost, for deeper beyond those sad eyes was an inability to silence the tormenting voices telling me I would turn out like my Dad.

It was hard for Kath, to stand by and watch her husband carry on this way—bent on self destruction. Yet, she tried her best, and in the practical things of life, she was my strength and carried me when I couldn't carry myself.

The Boy the Tree and the Trench

No matter how old you get,
the hole in your heart
created by your father's absence
still aches.[10]

To feel you've been dropped into a seething desert is one thing, but to link your suffering with prodigal issues is another. I had found the pigpen and wallowed in its mud. All alone, I cried, 'Help, get me out of here.' But such places are hard to escape when emotions are ignored. I told myself, *run as fast as you can.* Sadly, I ran smack-bang into the brushing aside of more horrid memories. There I continued to inebriate my pain. My worth was near zero, and I could not understand I was still valuable when everything around me was falling apart. It was hard to focus. The painful rhetoric made my head sore, even more so when everything had become all about me.

It is hard to see another's perspective when we are focusing on ourselves. I was unaware how Kath had been responding to my grief and how heartbroken she had become. To see the man of her dreams fall apart was devastating for her. Neither of us could calm the other down. Kath's anxiety peaked at the breakfast table, and unable to cope any longer, she was admitted to a psych ward in a large Sydney hospital where she tried to offload her fear that I might never recover.

My life had become utterly unmanageable, and I had been through a doozy by the time Kath eventually came

Chapter 8 - Home

home. Too drunk to think clearly, I contemplated suicide several times, but thankfully, I got a good taste of reality and made sure those feelings passed and never returned. Nonetheless, I was still very much out of sorts with myself, and those childhood weights of rejection still crushed my heart. Hypersensitive to loud noises, I felt my nerves were about to explode. I was jealous of everyone's successes and critical of everyone's faults. In the day-to-day things, I felt like a failure—a feeling I sensed had been with me ever since Dad had disappeared and Mum refused to talk about that.

I had a lot of stomach aches when I was a kid, and when the pain in my gut became too much, I was admitted to a local hospital. There I became an enigma. No one knew what to do with me. While they medically treated the duodenal ulcer, I was taken to the psych ward, where I promptly disappeared into the paperwork and became nothing more than a number.

9
Dad's Book

Have you ever wished your past could be hidden? So you could forget about it? I certainly have. If I could have hidden my Vietnam Service Ribbons at home, while managing the moratoriums as a cop, it would have been easier. But pinned on me, those ribbons incited abusive language from a rowdy mob—it was more than I could handle. I was struggling as it was, and this set me back quite a bit further. After a day battling a 30,000 complication on Sydney's narrow winding streets, I'd come home furiously upset at the slightest thing.

Kath couldn't keep up with my mood swings and would say to me, "You're back home from Vietnam. You should be happy." *Yeah, I should be happy,* I thought. But at night, I'd be awake battling intrusive thoughts and flashbacks. Most of the time, I would be up drinking, sad, still searching for a father that'd hold me during one of the worst times of my life. I had been underperforming and was overwhelmed–drinking became a war front fought out at home. I kept focusing on things that made me sad, and was sick of others not knowing the struggles I endured. The price of moving on with my life was high. To fix my heart, even higher. I knew that. While strolling through a shopping

Chapter 9 - Dad's Book

mall, I found a cap with "Freedom isn't free," embroidered on it. More than anything, having it sit close on my forehead was a cry for help. Freedom has many voices. For me, it spoke of being loved and known by a dad who cared for me. With no such support, and with memories, too close for comfort, it got too much, and again I was admitted to a nearby hospital and sent to a psychiatrist for assessment. "What's up with you, fella?" He asked. With my mask firmly in place, I replied, 'I'm fine.' After several visits, it came to a point where I refused to see the guy. He was a dead-set bozo, as good to me as a booby trap. *I'll show him when he wipes me off with, 'What's up, fella?' Right, I'll show you— nothing, that's what!* He heard from me what he wanted to hear, and upon my discharge, I threw his medication out the train window.

At home, my grief made everyone unhappy. My children did not deserve what I dished out to them—no way! I would ask myself, 'Was my behaviour justified?' I'd answer, 'No.' But I also didn't know what was happening to me. No one could tell me I had been locked into a situation that had almost destroyed me, or explain how it prevented me living my best life. Even so, I still had a lot to answer for with my erratic behaviour. My behaviour affected Kath in ways I never could imagine. Kath had known me as a husband who had given his heart and soul to her, so she couldn't understand why I could not be there for her. Kath felt the distance between us, and she needed someone to listen to her, but except for the occasional Vietnam veteran's wife, she had no one to understand what she had been going through. It was hard for Kath to socialise. Without me by her side, she began isolating herself. Withdrawing into herself had become her greatest hindrance. Kath had every reason to go and take the boys with her, but she didn't leave me.

With winter snow thawing and apple blossoms bursting pink, it was a perfect time to visit Armidale with my little family. There was an event at the Bowling Club, and Mum and Cyril worked together in the kitchen on the night. Excited to see me, Cyril took me aside and introduced me to every person in the nosily energetic dining room. "I want you to meet my son, Davey; he is back from Vietnam," he'd say. By the time we had finished saying hello, the coldness in my heart had given way to a warmth I barely knew was possible. To this day, Cyril remains a father figure who was there for me during some of my most heart-wrenching days.

In 1973 we were living in Sydney, and I was working in the Commonwealth Police Force, moving through the ranks into higher positions. When off duty, I kept in touch with Neville, my best mate, together, the two of us were rogues, risk-takers, and great drinking buddies. Nev was a one-in-a-million, the kindest bloke you'd ever meet. Over drinks, he'd help me shake off the effects of those horrible years at war and he seemed broken-hearted I couldn't move forward. I well remember the autumn day my world

Chapter 9 - Dad's Book

completely crashed. At Nev's place, over a few beers and tea for the girls, he told us their news. "We are packing up and moving to Queensland." Neville's leaving was the last straw for me, and it was hardly a joke that my best mate was moving interstate. I took it personally and didn't speak to him for a long time.

Months later, I was on my way home from the town mall. Ever since that autumn day, tension had been building within me. Frustration had now peaked, and while approaching some traffic lights, I stuck my head out the window and screamed, 'When is all of this going to stoppp?'

"Neverrrr! Get used to itttt!!" Came the brazen reply from a passenger who'd stuck his head out of the car cruising up alongside me.

Drongo, what would he know?

I was more troubled than ever as my car pulled into the driveway. Kath and I were at each other's throats, cascading toward imminent divorce. I felt lost, furiously so, and I couldn't say I liked watching my marriage dissolve before my eyes. I knew I had a lot of work to do to fix my heart, yet I still didn't have the skills.

With Nev gone, it was time to revisit the book that had been patched together in my mind about my Dad. I flipped the first page over to when Kath and I had pulled up outside the hospital. We had not long been married and as newlyweds followed a nurse down a long corridor into a cold room. A chill went up my spine when I spotted a white-haired man slumped over in his chair. Drawing a deep breath I said to him, 'Hello, I am your oldest son, the one you abandoned.' Trying to douse my rising anger, I continued, 'You left us four kids to fend for ourselves thirty-odd years ago.' He straightened himself, and looked away, and briefly said something, as if awkwardly muttering to himself, "Yeah, I am William Poulton."

Kath tried to patch things up, but I gently drew her arm close, and we turned and walked towards the door. I retraced my steps to the car and mused, *I've finally caught up with you, Mum's big secret. How convenient, you were the one who gave me wings, but it barely matters now. You almost ruined my life and left me with a massive wound in my heart and a hole so deep that no amount of love from others could fill it. You took away my blue sky, and I flew alone into a dark abyss*. My heart sank, and I wiped my watery eyes and drove off.

> Forgive yourself for believing something was lacking in you because he wasn't there.
> (Vanzant, 2020).[11]

In the next chapter, I read from Dad's Service Record. He had constantly gotten drunk while serving in the Middle East, and had behaved in a disorderly fashion in

Chapter 9 Dad's Book

the trenches. He was often Absent Without Official Leave and had been continually punished with hefty fines and no pay. His defiant and unruly lifestyle spoke of a disbelief in himself. Like my Dad, who had made a mess of his life, I was sure making a great mess of mine. My Dad had lost his way, and I struggled to find my way forward. I remember condemning myself as a right drongo.

> And I hate how you
> made me question myself
> when the problem was you all along.[12]

I closed the last chapter when I learned Dad's best mate had been killed in the war, and he had gone to visit the grieving widow and fell in love with her. "Skeletons come out eventually," said Uncle Blue and, even the golden chest echoed, "I've kept it a secret, the truth of this woman and their six children together until you could tolerate the pain of it." My father was a stranger. To attend his funeral as an estranged son was not my style. When invited, I thought, *no, I have already said my goodbyes to him*. With that closure –a goodbye also to the tremendous unrest this had created in my soul. I let my dad go. But I still needed a father who'd walk me into the things of manhood and show me bravery without brutality and purpose without running everyone into the ground to get it.

PART THREE

My motto –

Be my own man and live my life my way.
People will let you down; never need them.

10
Ambushed

Kath and I were having a horrid time getting on, and it was that year we decided to split. We were fixing the house to sell, and then we had planned on going our separate ways, happily for both of us. We were in the middle of renovating, I was cursing and swearing in the bathroom, and Kath added to the torrential storm with her angry replies when the doorbell rang. Covered in concrete dust and at the height of one of our heated exchanges, I called out, "Kath answer the door!" Moments later, my old mate poked his head inside the bathroom. "G'day, mate, how's it all going?"

Happy to see that cheeky face, I said, 'Nev, I would have stocked up if I knew you were coming. A good yarn over a Black Label would help right now.'

Neville's eyes locked onto mine, "I've given up the drink. Something more powerful helps me now. God told us to come and take you, Kath, and the boys back to Queensland with us. What do you say? Interested in coming up for a holiday?"

'Spose,' I muttered, 'but Kath won't come. We can't stand being in the same room anymore, and we yell between the walls at each other.' Nev looked at me with a hope I had not seen in a long while and said, "Don't worry about Kath; Helen is in there right now with her." Kath was all in and began packing the Volkswagen with pillows and blankets. Just after midnight, my hands bounced off the steering wheel in the subzero cold and our young sons settled. After an initial engine splutter, we were off down the street and out onto the highway.

Everything would have been fine except for the low-lying mist in the new direction we had taken. Kath and I took turns driving, and even with the high-powered driving lights, the narrow twists and turns made it all such a nervous adventure. Eventually, we pulled into MacDonald's for breakfast, and by daylight, we had crossed the Queensland border. I thought about where our marriage had taken us. We had reached rock bottom, and we both had severe Post-Traumatic Stress Disorder, something neither of us were handling. Our constant bickering had put a wedge between us and our growing boys.

Kath had always been my sweetheart; I just needed to be better within myself. Yet, at Ipswich, I felt so lost. Completely and utterly lost, with no way of feeling safe within myself. I was out of my depth with no obvious way forward. Both Kath and I were drowning in our mess.

Neville's home felt like a monastery, what with their kids actually liking each other and their constant chatter about Jesus. "There is a charismatic meeting at a Catholic

Chapter 10 - Ambushed

church on Friday night, we want you to come," Nev kept saying. I thought *if I agreed, they'd stop harassing me*. And besides, I was sick of the cold war Kath and I were battling out.

After dinner on the Friday, Nev, our wives, and I piled into my VW Beetle and began driving up to Bardon. Nev was in the front with me, Helen in the back with Kath, who happily went along with everything. I felt the odd one out as I sat there tolerating Nev's constant chatter about God. I tried being polite but honestly, it became too much, and I slammed on the brakes! With the smell of burnt rubber filling the car, and fumes vibrating off me, I turned to them and with angry eyes, yelled, 'If you don't stop talking to me about God and Jesus, you can all get to the meeting some other way. I am taking the keys and driving off without you lot!'

"OK, Helen," ordered Nev, "You're in the front with Dave, and I'll sit in the back with Kath. I promise I won't talk to you about Jesus for the rest of the trip. Not to you, at least. I promise."

'Fine!' I snapped. 'Just make sure you don't,' and then I spun the back wheels and drove off. In the silence, I could hear myself fuming. By the time we arrived and had parked the car I had calmed down. Inside the meeting, the place was buzzing, and the energy danced around me, almost saying, "You too can be part of this." In a crowd of about 500 people, I nodded to some close by me, and Nev picked out some seats and placed me in the middle of the row. The two nuns sitting in front of me turned and smiled and at the sound of drums, everyone got to their feet and began singing. After the priest gave his sermon, an ordinary looking guy stepped to the microphone. A hush fell over the room as he looked out over the congregation and in a deep voice said, "Here tonight are two groups of people. To both, God asks, Who AM I?" At that point, both Nuns turn and nod as if to say, "He is talking to you." I ignored their brazen smiles and, under my breath, replied, *Dumb question, it doesn't apply to me! You don't exist, so who cares?*

The second question God asks, Who Am I to you?" I am getting further upset at the nuns and again thought, *Don't care, you don't exist*! I began squirming; *What is he up to? And who does he think he is?* I shook my head, *Why am I answering these questions? I must be losing the plot! I bet Nev put this joker up to this!*

Finally, God asks, "What are you to Me?" Unable to hold it in any longer, the torrential pain in my heart gushed out. Loud enough for everyone to hear, I yelled, 'A bloody nuisance, that's what I am to God.' Nev and Kath glared at me, as if to say, "Don't you dare make a scene!" I felt their fear, yet became distracted by a noise, as if a bee had nosedived my ear and hovered over it. Kath leaned over

Chapter 10 - Ambushed

and whispered, "I can smell roses, can you?" Come to think about it, *yes*, and the scent became noticeably stronger as she spoke. The bee-like sound hovering over my ear went inside me, and, as if in a science fiction moment, it began drilling into the old emotional chest-tightening wound of all those years ago. With a touch of heat, the gentle sensation loosened some of that pain. It was an unforgettable moment— one I'd always remember.

At the invitation, I pushed past tethered knees, jumped over the dividing altar rail, and raced into the vestry. While holding some coffee, I told them about that bizarre moment and reflected upon my life-long belief that a God of love could possibly not exist— what with all the suffering in the world. But then I said, 'Everything changed for me. Was I ready? No, I was not. Was I shocked? Absolutely. Yet I felt that supernatural experience to be the most natural thing ever. Those heavy weights had lifted; I feel so light I could float.'

Everything seemed different on the drive home—the air seemed fresher and the stars brighter. Kath and Helen were in the back singing, and in the front next to me was my best mate Nev, chatting to me about God. I had gone to the meeting upset and angry and came away praising the One I had earlier cursed. 'God must have known the only the way He could get to me was to ambush me, completely take me off guard and overwhelm my heart in an explosion of love.'

Nev agreed, "It was the only way He could get you to come home." With great warmth, Helen said, "It will take time to become familiar with your new life, but we are here to help you process your new identity as His child."

One thing though, said Nev, "Life is going to be a big adventure for you, and you'll get more healing as you go along." I replied, 'Finally, I can understand what you both had been drilling me with – Jesus had died for me so I could live a life free from the weights and bondages of the past. I get it now and understand that I am not here to stay stuck in my mud but to find the One who was slain for me, the Lamb of God, my Redeemer.'

I had *never* felt this happy, and certainly, it was a welcomed relief from the years of heartache I had endured. As I turned into their driveway that late night hour, a deep contentment filled my soul.

11
New Adventures

Some memories never leave you, and the next morning I woke with that inner fire still warming my soul. After breakfast, Nev thought I was joking when I said, 'Let's go to the pub.' By the look on his face, he wasn't sure about that! But we went anyway, 'Everyone should know about this,' I told him.

I had been in these sorts of pubs plenty of times before. But I had never gone in there and not needed a drink. I gathered a few blokes around me and told of the ambush and was startled to see hope rising within them. I saw a hunger in their eyes and could hear the desperation in their voices. I had never heard voices the way I did that day. 'The meeting is tonight,' I told them. 'But be willing for anything to happen,' I said.

My best mate then gave me a Bible, and after reading some of it, I could feel my heart climbing down from the pine tree that I had hidden myself in since my Armidale days. Instead, a different Tree, the eternal age-old Calvary Cross became my hiding place and its eternal Arms of love were waiting to hold me somewhere in my future.

The Boy the Tree and the Trench

I had gone to Queensland for a holiday and came back with a new life. My early days persisting with guitar lessons paid off, and I was invited to join the music band at church. At the time (1974), we attended a charismatic prayer group at the bishop's residence in Hurstville. I had become familiar with God's voice, in private, at least. Then one day, He blatantly showed up when I was out with friends. In one of the Friday night prayer meetings, the lead guitarist, in a room full of loud music, heard what I thought was someone whispering to me. I looked around, but there was no one. I continued playing, and heard the whispering again, it was distinctly louder this time. So I listened. It was a message for the group. It scared the living daylights out of me–I thought I was going mad. So I asked the invisible voice, 'Why are you picking on me?' I then said, 'Go and pick on someone else.'

My guitar pic had barely touched the strings again when I knew they were loose. At a quick glance, the keys were unwinding before my eyes. Right out of the *Twilight Zone,* the voice whispered, "Have I got your attention now? Go and do as I have asked." I put the guitar down and tapped the leader on his shoulder. He turned to me and annoyingly asked, "What is it, Dave?" I cleared my throat and perked up the courage to say, 'I have a message for the group, which appears to be from God.' With a fit of anger in his eyes, he said, "Go back and get your guitar and continue playing." I lamented, 'I can't; my guitar strings are now loose.' I turned

Chapter 11 - New Adventures

to walk away, only to be stopped by the assistant leader. "Just a minute Dave." He swung back around and said to the skeptical leader, "Look, if it is the Holy Spirit, I don't want to be the disobedient one."

"OK, let him bring it. We will see if it is the Holy Spirit or not." I told everyone about the strange experience. How I had watched the strings become loose. Then I told them what God had said to me. To my surprise, the whole place erupted, and the leaders received the news as a rebuke. I turned to walk away when the main leader stood up. "You have heard from the Holy Spirit. Dave, I want to ask your forgiveness for doubting you. You have the Spirit of the Lord within you, and you have the mind of Christ. Who am I to question who God will use and who He won't."

As I packed away my guitar later that night, I told God that He was not to *ever* do that to me again. But did He listen? No, for many other times I heard His voice speak. While it was always relevant, it was nerve-wracking because I wanted to be seen as an average bloke, just like everyone else. My need to belong and fit in with everyone else became my greatest challenge to overcome.

Secretly, we do want to hear God speak. Yet, it scares us. So, we close our ears and embrace a theoretical approach that keeps us in the wilderness. Yet, folk, even in churches, live in dry wilderness places. Even there, many do not respond to God's voice; instead, they stand at a distance.

Months later, I was at a Parish Council Meeting and casually mentioned that Jesus was my friend. They were outraged. The presiding President said, "That's blasphemy; Jesus is High and lofty, not your friend." I remember thinking *they have totally missed the point and have no idea about a love-sick God who wants to be our friend.* From that point on, religion became the bane of my life. I saw it as an institution existing solely to argue theoretical viewpoints. And to me, those of the cloth seemed more informed about divine realities than God Himself. For them, it was "what" you knew, not "Who" you knew. It had nothing to do with friendship with God or loving Him or being patient and kind to others. Religion to them was an intellectual exercise, a theoretical contest, a race to the top of the class! And for Kath and I, it was a life of faith, we just wanted a rose garden and a path and Someone to walk alongside us on it. But only classrooms could be found in that church.

As part of the Commonwealth Police Force, I was tasked to write Regional Bomb Response Procedures, for which I was given a Commissioners Commendation for Diligence. I couldn't have been happier, even with the monotonous routine — just a lot of paperwork. But then, a catastrophe changed everything for me. It occurred in the early months of 1978 when, at the time, I had been on duty for bomb detection and rapid response at a highly acclaimed hotel in the city. The nightlife had been grinding to a halt in the early morning hours when a compactor in

Chapter 11 - New Adventures

a garbage truck activated, causing a bomb in the back to detonate. Three people were sadly killed, and eleven others injured. Over the next few days, my boss had me clear all the garbage bins in the streets and bordering hotels. It was a nerve-wracking time. My nervous system was on high alert, and even when transferred further south of the city, I still needed to feel safe. Kath was keenly aware of my grief and that I was finding it hard even to let God's love calm my emotions. I encouraged her, 'Keep on with the big job of raising our family.'

My abilities in handling bomb-related incidents earned me a stack of promotions and a new job in Canberra. It was not an easy move for Kath, for she had made a great life for herself and our boys in Sydney. Eventually, a reluctant wife joined me and we found a new church. It was small, but not religious. In fact, the nineteen others there also wanted a genuine relationship with God.

The congregation grew substantially, and we stayed there for many years. I became *au fait* with my Spiritual gifts and learned quickly to obey God's inner promptings. Many people in dire situations were touched by God's power. As much as we loved the people, painful push-back assignments had been set against me. I took these situations to Jesus and complained. He gently but very firmly said, "I do not incite or create evil upon your life— nor do I sit around thinking, who can I hurt next (the devil does that!) I died a cruel death at the hand of religion so I could make you my own. Yet, though I have taken back the keys to Hell and Hades, the world still lies in the grasp of evil, and will do so until the end of time. I want you to know, what happened to you was not Me; that came from man's unbelieving heart, not My heart of faith. Try not to let anything discourage you or derail your trust in Me. It is your responsibility to love everybody and pray for my protection. I will always wrap your heart up in Mine if you allow Me to heal you."

God had reached out to me and clearly shown me His love. Yet, unhealed traumas, a broken heart, knocked confidence and scant sense of belonging would continue have me living in wilderness places and perhaps even, prevent me from escaping the orphan spirit.

Canberra had clean air and relatively few high-rise buildings. Yet, the roads were a convoluted matrix of twists and turns that were hard to follow, especially on dark wintry nights. As a consultant to the Australian Government, I made hard-to-grasp concepts simple and ably turned high-level complexities into accessible data. I also became part of the Australian Federal Police Bomb Response Unit and assisted in training the State Police in Bomb disposal techniques. I couldn't have been happier with my feet firmly planted in this new direction. Yet it was a hectic time in my life, and amid the pressures, I felt fragile, worn out, and, most of all, stuck in my own personal mud.

12
Awoken

My personal issues and other unresolved wartime memories still had a big hold on me. Yet, despite the trauma, another part of me had moved forward. We had settled into the suburb of Duffy and had become used to the freezing winters there. And one of those below-zero mornings, I had awoken to a familiar male voice calling my name. My hand fumbled towards the bedside lamp, I switched on the light and opened my eyes to an empty room. I snuggled into my pillow and thought, *I must be going mad.* I heard the voice again, and I woke Kath.

She sleepily asked, "Was my name mentioned?"

'No, only mine.'

"Fine, I am going back to sleep," then rolled over.

Great help that was, I thought. Hoping He'd hear, I whispered, 'Was that you, Jesus?' Instantly, with a greater insistence, the voice replied. "Read Colossians, chapter one, verse twenty-one through to the end." *It must be God*, I mused. *But why? Was I in trouble?* Being in trouble was the norm for me, so that was another reason for my nervousness as I began reading.

The Boy the Tree and the Trench

Once, you were alienated from God and were enemies in your mind because of your evil behaviour. But now He has reconciled you by Christ's physical body through death to present you holy in His sight, without blemish, free from accusation if you continue in your faith.

The reading, as it continued, surprisingly was an invitation to teach what I had been learning. *Hmm, a new direction; I better take this down the street and show these scriptures to the Senior Minister.*

He was stunned. "Well, if it is God, it will come to pass." He might not have meant for me to hear his cynical tone, but I did hear it. I couldn't blame him either. After all, no one else heard the voice and I could have been making the entire story up for all he knew.

Culturally, we were at a crossroads. The media had not yet ramped up its rhetoric, but women were heading out of their homes in droves for a new life at the office. Even churches were slipping into secular ways and were pushing spiritual things into the background. Indeed, a voice, an invisible voice at that, did not fit in with a post-modern world. God knew what He was up against, and He knew it could interfere with His plans. However, I knew He was trying to reach deeper into my soul.

I enrolled as an audit student at the Canberra Theological College to give this new direction a chance.

Chapter 12 Awoken

It was a start. Spencer Sutherland took me under his wing and gave me a solid grounding in study methodology. He said, "If you have a powerful study method, you will have a powerful ministry." How true that was. Spencer was supportive in every sense of the word. His expertise and intimate knowledge of Scripture made studying more straightforward than I first thought. He gave me private tuition to help me catch up on the lectures I had missed because of my specialist job. I was given incredible support and had found my niche, yet there was still a lot of dread and angst in me concerning a God who punishes little kids. I found it near impossible to get past my childhood belief, the trauma prevented me moving forward.

Due to the high level of fitness required for Police work, I had to recuperate longer than usual after a complicated knee reconstruction and health issues relating to that operation. This gave me ample time to study. It also gave some welcomed time for Mum to visit us. Mum loved Canberra, and she especially enjoyed spending time with her grandchildren. Our boys loved their Nan spoiling them.

Kath and I also had some wonderful late-night chats with Mum. I could see her gentle determination to give everything she had so we could be happy. It was on one of those nights, in a rare moment, Mum told us that she had always hoped Dad would return. With this belief and her devotion to her Catholic lifestyle, she refused to divorce and remarry. We spent hours into the night, reminiscing on the 1950's— a time when cultural rhetoric frowned on almost everything outside the norm, "Tut-tut," it would say. I sat across from Mum and admired her staunch resolute. Even her friends, work colleagues and neighbours admired her push-back and held her in high regard as they watched Mum bravely weather a tough life. Mum mused, "It was pretty difficult pushing against the hard economic and social values metered against me." Kath and I agreed. I especially admired her ability to keep our family together, and her focus on giving us a good name and remaining faithful to us kids. In retrospect, I can't ever remember anyone describing our family as dysfunctional.

At her funeral, I reflected upon her good heart and realised her ability to cope as a deserted wife manifested in misdirected anger. Whilst she was a veritable tyrant with us kids, I stood at her coffin and thanked her for doing her best and never giving up on her children.

13
The Miracle

Wonderfully, before Mum passed away, our relationship continued to blossom.

But still, the brokenness inside me still needed fixing. After reading about Apollyon in the book of Revelations, I thought *Yep, I know about that, for indeed, we have been caught up in all sorts of mental conflicts.* Since meeting Jesus, I have also experienced the good Shepherd. I read how He had left the ninety-nine to find the one that had gone off and had gotten lost. No matter how lost we have become, a search party will always be sent out.

Kath and I created a tight-knit home group, and as their leader, I discovered I could be part of that search and rescue team. It was on a Saturday afternoon (I have changed the names of those in our Home Fellowship Group to protect their privacy). I answered the phone to a frantic voice telling me, "Dave, my mother has gone crazy and has locked herself in the house. Can you please come and find my mother and see if she is alright?"

As I drove there, I prayed, 'Lord, I don't know what has happened, but You do. Give me the wisdom to know what to do. Father, in Jesus' name, I bind the enemy's work in this family. Satan, you will not have the victory!' I had barely finished praying that prayer when I drove up around the corner to find everyone standing on the road outside their house. They were glad to see me and to have someone be with them during this stressful time. I asked them. 'So, tell me what's going on.'

"We had a huge fight, and my mother went crazy, yelling and screaming, and it scared me. I have never seen her like this before. You know we are a fiery lot, but this...."

'Where did you last see your mother?' I asked.

"In the kitchen. We all just took off. Here is the key to the house. Dave, you know us all; my mother respects you. She will talk to you."

I searched every room, calling her name, but no Karla. No one. I came back into the main bedroom on the first floor. As I was about to leave, my eye caught sight of a pair of shoes between the bed and the window, just noticeable with the heels showing. I went over, and Karla was lying on the floor with a belt tied around her neck, fastened to the bedpost. Her skin had turned bluish colour, and her eyes didn't respond. I couldn't find a pulse. It was then that the son-in-law Tom walked in. He confirmed that she had gone. I was about to ring the police operations when the Holy Spirit said, "What are you doing?" I replied, 'Phoning the death in.' As clear as a bell, the Holy Spirit said, "This is

Chapter 13 The Miracle

not unto death." Tom held a postmodern belief that God had died and we were alone in the universe. But he was impressed by my love for him and my faith in God and had been searching a similar reality. He was all the more fascinated when I told him, 'I am going to pray and tell the spirit of death to leave this house now!' I knelt and placed my hand on Karla's forehead, and commanded the spirit of death to leave the house and never return. Suddenly, there was an almighty gasp as Karla took a deep breath. She sat up, looked at me, and said, "Padre Dave, will you make me a cup of tea?"

I thought, *Yes, absolutely Karla, but first let me catch my breath.* It's not everyday someone comes back from the dead like that! And in disbelief, Tom struggled. I had already seen God do many out-of-the-box things, but I guess for both of us, we were utterly astonished. Even though startled, I managed to make us all a pot of tea. I returned to the room and helped Karla onto the edge of the bed. She sipped her tea, and I asked her to tell me what had happened.

"A bright light drew me down a long corridor, and I came out on what appeared to be a massive walkway. Thousands of people were streaming past the most brilliant Man I had ever seen. When I went to pass Him, He crossed His arms, looked down, and said, "You can't come in here; you must go back and change your filthy rags." Everything went black, and I woke up with you kneeling beside me." I sat there, grateful to see Karla's smile. She had been the backbone of her family and I was curious to know why despair had gotten the upper hand. I had to ask the obvious question, 'What was going on for you?'

"I didn't want to kill myself," she said, "But I had to escape all the fighting in the family. I couldn't cope with it anymore. I just wanted to get away from it all." I turned to Tom, 'Can you phone every family member and tell them what has happened? Get them all up here.' I mused on all that God had said to me previously and certainly I was grateful to be part of God's strategic plans for my friends.

An hour later, Karla's family happily gathered in her lounge room and a remarkable reconciliation had taken place. By one o'clock the following morning, God had done a mighty work. Tom put his faith in Jesus and began his own adventure with God. Yet, Jesus wasn't finished with this family, and to this day, they still see me as their pastor and regularly pop in to visit Kath and me.

14
Piercing Eyes

I thrived on the love of these beautiful people. In this environment, I felt energetic and alive.

I had been away from home for several months, assisting high-level officials in bomb analysis and I felt something wasn't right. Perhaps it was nothing more than I just hadn't seen Kath and the kids for a while. It had also been a while since I felt the warmth of happy friends at church. Take your soul out of that environment for a time, and you will feel lost.

I had set up training sessions in Bomb disposal techniques and made many new friends in those courses. I had become highly respected within the ranks and felt as if I had reached the epitome of manhood. Though highly successful, I had hoped a social life would fill the empty space inside me. But even a social life was not enough, for my internal need to feel uniquely special had created a vacuum in my life. I felt so alone I thought I'd lose my breath. Neither my family or God had been there for me when I was a kid, and I sensed the catching of my breath came from feeling abandoned. Instead of calling home and engaging in some tender words with Kath to fill the void, I decided not to bother her. I had not given God much thought either. Just as my Dad had done, I too, was a son off in a faraway land, searching for my own life. It was a small matter in my eyes, but I had grown up with small things turning into gigantic bombshells. I heard a voice from the past, "The walls you built are too high; you cannot escape."

Because Dad had neglected me, I worried I could not lead my boys as a father would lead them. Facing this within myself was like walking into a furnace of pain.

The weekend had just passed, and still, I had not checked in with my family. It had slipped my mind again to call. On the Monday, I was sitting at my desk, sorting through some correspondence, when I was interrupted with, "What do you think you are doing?" I knew that voice. It was God. And I knew His question had nothing to do with the piles of paper on my desk. From the sound of it, God wasn't impressed I had ignored my family obligation. It mattered, and He focused His gaze upon me.

Missing my family was not a big thing to me, but ignoring them, according to God, was huge. Instead of being mad at me, astonishingly, His question came with a sense of compassion, "My heart is still open to you."

I phoned Kath and happily left a message on the answering machine. She didn't call back, and I felt justified that she was busy and didn't need my checking in on her. But no. Kath would have liked me to show her that I cared

Chapter 14 Piercing Eyes

more than I had, and I regretted the ache I had put them through —a family who had faithfully stood by me and deserved to feel secure and loved. Later that week, I called up one of my close and respected friends and told him about my dilemma. 'God asked me a question, and it's one I do not want to answer.'

"Sounds like you are going through a tough time."

'Yeah,' I said. 'Even though I've reached great heights in my work, I feel stuck inside a wringer.'

My friend knew of my upbringing. He called again and said, "It is all about epigenetics. If you are worried you'll turn out like your Dad, it will become your internal narrative and, in the right situation, will surface, and become your reality." The insight helped me understand the matrix I had become caught up in. 'I guess my fear had gotten me tangled,' I replied. In it all, I felt challenged to make things right with Kath and my boys. At the very least, I'd commit to calling my family twice a week when working away from home.

Even so, I was still reeling with a self-loathing that was hard to process. Have you ever been through a tough time and have beaten yourself up because you did not have wherewithal to get through that situation? Being hard on ourselves is a social construct. It is something more than one teacher has taught us. For those who relate, our greatest challenge is showing patience and kindness to ourselves. I needed to give myself some tenderheartedness and forgive myself for becoming caught up in Mum's view of things. This would not be easy, for the trauma of her words had created a scenario whereby I had been living a double life —spic and span on the outside and a mess on the inside. It's very common with us blokes, and mostly the discrepancies are not resolved until our core pain is dealt with.

God had made it clear that He wanted a deeper relationship with me and had not abandoned me. Even so, I held myself back, for I was not thoroughly convinced of my value as a son in this world. My father abandoned me, so where does that leave me? Will God also abandon me? Theoretically, we may have a lot of information about God's view of us, but the information does not change us if we do little with it. I knew God to be loving and even heard He was a loving Father. But none of that had ever changed me, for it was still only theory – stuck in my head. I longed for this knowledge to reach my heart, for I knew only when it had, would God become the Father I had always wanted.

15
Living the Dream

Most young boys dream of becoming heroic. I certainly dreamt of being a hero in uniform, directing people toward doing the right thing. Seriously, people needed my help when I was a kid, and if I had been a policeman then, I might have come down very hard on one or two in Armidale and given some hefty fines.

Much later in life, I began living that dream, yet my heart had become a lot softer. I remember the night I had been driving up to Woden while on duty. It was dark and misty yet clear enough to see a car up ahead, almost running off the road. I put my siren on and pulled him over. He looked drunk, and immediately I checked in with God to get His assessment of the situation. I then asked the gentleman a few questions and decided to see if God's answer was correct, so I put my head a little inside the window and asked him, 'Sir, would you be suffering from a migraine headache right now?'

The gentleman looked at me in disbelief and answered, "Yes, I am getting flashes of light." I then offered to pray for his headache, which I did, and he immediately began feeling better. I walked away, thankful that now I had a softer heart and a more profound sense of fairness.

The Boy the Tree and the Trench

When I saw the pain in the eyes of young lads who had been brought in for being ratbags, I thought back to when I had lived without a father's warmth and direction. Like me, many of these young men had been traumatized by not having a dad to hold them. Without those strong arms, it's easy to feel punished by life.

Many of my workmates were Christians, and we got together and formed a Christian Support Group to encourage these boys and become aware of their pain and frustration. We'd introduce the Creator God to them. "He knows you and waits for the day you'll return from your wanderings." Most liked the idea of having a safe place to feel protected from the storms of life. We'd provide handwritten warnings without charges and then reconcile them with their parents. We saw that as effective policing.

We, in the support group had been actively involved in these young lives for a short while when, over a chat, a Detective Inspector said, "You know, the monthly arrest statistics are quite low now. It is because you are helping those boys!" Of course, my mates and I were happy to hear that. It proved belonging and being seen and heard are what boys need the most. Yet our influence did not impress the diehards, and they kept ensuring we knew that.

My next transfer was a fulfillment of another of my childhood dreams. Let's back up a bit to when I had played with explosives at high school. It never occurred that God

Chapter 15 Living the Dream

cared about me, especially when that bomb in the quadrangle had almost exploded in my face. My science teacher knew explosives naturally intrigued me. But he did not know I wanted to learn how to disarm them safely. Now in my new job, I was given this chance. Many times, in fact. To disarm bombs, I had to walk into dangerous situations and this had some of my colleagues feeling like nervous wrecks.

I had not yet learned to trust God with my emotional pain. But it was imperative I trust Him to protect my life from danger while working in a Specialist Unit, handling bomb-related incidents. And, to trust explicitly, after numerous bombs had exploded near a busy shopping center. It was Christmastime. Any sort of mishap during that frantic time of year is difficult enough. But the days were particularly tenuous, for we had no knowledge of where or when a bomb would explode next. With a rare confidence, I'd walk onto these sites with a calm persona. When I'd linger longer than necessary though, my mates felt nervous. Months later, having understood the truth of what happened, I built a prototype component with my know-how and ability.

Shortly afterward, I flew to the United Kingdom on other police business. While there, I took opportunity to brief the New Scotland Yard Counter Terrorist unit. Even overseas, I had gotten myself the reputation as the Aussie Cop who was the safest bloke to be around after a bomb explosion. Each day I'd remind myself of Psalm 91 and that, and other scriptures, kept my faith strong. I built, with God's Word, internal structures that nothing on earth could shatter. My mates dubbed my courage as a superpower.

On my return to Australia, I was invited to a conference in New Zealand. There, I delivered a keynote address to the delegates on our findings. I was lapping up the attention on center stage. But that attention fell into the wrong hands, and those hands drew a target on my back.

I knew divine protection was mine. But not everyone saw the situation from my perspective. Ultimately they thought I needed to escape the situation and I was transferred from my Specialty Unit into an office job back at the headquarters.

16
The Mystery Meeting

The traffic was moderately heavy on my first day driving to the headquarters, and the brewed coffee gave me the spark I needed as I sat chatting with my new colleagues. The next day, before leaving home and after a comforting chat with Kath at the breakfast table, I asked God, 'What are You and I going to get up to today?" I had always asked God that question and knew His answer would include some sort of adventure.

The airy, high-windowed office made it a pleasant room and an inspiring workplace. While sipping a relished coffee on my second day at work, I felt God say, "I want to spend thirty minutes each morning with you, we have lots to discuss." That afternoon, I found a sign and from then on, each morning I'd slip it over the antique knob, and close the heavy door behind me. I then sank into my leather chair.

Engaging heaven and getting God's perspective was a lot of fun. One time, I had been gazing out the window. I was pondering on the situation out there, not staring at anything in particular, when I felt God say to look harder. With my binoculars He showed me something that had been on the agenda at last week's squad meeting. At the time, Canberra had a lot of underground stuff going on, and God enabled me to see a problematic situation that we had been unable to solve. Those thirty minutes meeting made my new job easier and definably exciting.

Unbeknown to me, my colleagues were intrigued by the *Meeting in Progress, Do not Disturb* sign and after months of suspense, sent a policewoman to investigate. I invited her into my office and, unannounced, she blurted out, "We all know you have a meeting before work, but at the thirty-minute mark, we watch that doorknob turn and see you emerge. But no one else comes out with you. We are wondering what is going on?"

In the staff tea room, this policewoman had rarely heard ideas around hearing God's voice or other such religious rhetoric. But I had no choice and told her anyway. 'During that thirty-minute meeting, I set my course for the day, and God speaks to me.' She tried to stop her face from falling off altogether and exclaimed, "So that is why you know so much about what is happening out there. Can I tell the others?"

The Inspector was the first to make his way to my office. "I am aware you have strategies that solve issues you should know nothing about," he said. I tried to convince him of the importance of the meetings but he was determined to stop them. Though a Catholic himself, he ordered me to keep religion out of the office environment. The thing is, I had caught hold of God's passion for this world, and nothing in

Chapter 16- The Mystery Meeting

heaven or hell could prevent it from absorbing my heart. Soon afterward, I retired from the Police Force and began a new job as a Pastor. I was looking forward to walking with God into a future adventure with Him.

At the farewell afternoon tea, the Assistant Commissioner said with a big smile, "Sergeant, I suppose tomorrow we will have to call you reverend?"

'Sir, I have been both sergeant and reverend simultaneously. I have been able to, with God's help, serve the people of the Australian Capital Territory and God with all diligence and dignity.' The day before retiring I threw a lot of things out from my desk, but I kept my small door sign as a bookmark and as a reminder of the fun I had during those thirty minute meetings, sitting with God each morning. It became very obvious that God knew everything about everyone and this was exactly what I needed to know for my next step of faith.

17
Ministry God's Way

To cope with the drama of being a fatherless kid, I complied to popular opinion. But even in my adult years I kept adapting my attitude and behaviour to suit what others wanted. Even after my encounter with God, when I no longer had to wing it alone, conforming was still an issue. But I hoped in this new workplace, all that might change.

My new job as a pastor brought a lot of joy to my heart. Though I had a stack of theological degrees including a Masters in Biblical Studies I promised myself I would make hearing God's voice precedent and the urgent would have to wait. To do this, I would quieten my heart and listen for heaven to speak.

Boys, especially, but other young adults also, viewed me as a father figure, and would ask complex questions. One time an older boy came to me looking sad and feeling sorry for himself. He said, "I have no value to God, so why would God even listen to me." I was about to answer when God interrupted me with, "Give the young boy a twenty dollar note." I took it out from my wallet and then I felt God say, "There's something about his question that's pulling on My heart strings. Ask him how much that note is worth." The boy answered twenty dollars. I then heard God tell me

Chapter 17- Mininstry God's Way

to say, 'If I were to destroy that note so that it was barely identifiable, what would the note be worth then?' The young voice answered, "I guess it would still be worth twenty dollars." I waited a few minutes for that reality to sink in, then said, 'So, this means the twenty dollar note does not lose its value even when bad things happen to it?'

"Yes, I guess so," he sheepishly said. I waited again. In the silence, I could feel God's tender heart for this young boy. 'God says you are like the twenty dollar note in that your value will never be lost no matter what happens to you.' Amid tears he answered, "But you don't know what I have been through." My deeply caring eyes met his downcast look, 'Over a chat, we can talk about that if you'd like. God knows the hell you have been through and has told me to tell you that you are precious to Him and He has a special place in His heart just for you.'

Finding happiness was a childhood quest, and these sorts of conversations made my life blissfully happy. I enjoyed knowing God would answer everyone's questions. In the busyness of that environment, I looked unbothered. Some seemed unnerved by that, and brought this into the spotlight and said, "Things have to be done around here our way. Asking God questions is not one of our ways." I was heartbroken. Instead of doing ministry God's way, I had to conform to their way of doing things. The entire situation felt like a heavy weight on my shoulders, and eventually I felt worn down by it all. I had no choice in the matter. I found myself working hard to get everyone's approval. It was easy to do. For most of my life, I had strived to be accepted. At a high level of performance, I complied with the status quo, and became a respected pastor. People looked up to me.

Mind you, that I enjoyed people's appraisals showed I still had issues concerning my worth as a son. Here is my story about that. While I performed at a high level, inside me something more sinister was going on. The love I craved while kicking the soccer ball around with my brothers had only intensified. Especially in a church, we expect to be loved. I grew up with a filter that I don't have the love I need. At the core of all human failing is a self-belief. I still believed I was inwardly flawed and no one cared. Carrying shame while, at the same time, working hard to find a name for myself was disastrous.

There was still a desire to be noticed. Those old ways of striving were still with me, and I was even more determined to be admired, appreciated and valued for simply who I was—not for what I could do. I wanted human love, the sort that would fancify my aching heart. To retain this love we men need a strong foundation; a bottom line that can withstand the knocks of life. Our foundations can easily be shaken by storms or crumble under pressure. We hide this weak point and bravely face the world as if we are superman. I know. My cape had fallen off and I have lost it when I had

Chapter 17 - Ministry God's Way

felt fragile and unsure of myself in relationships. Perhaps this admission might surprise those who expect a great deal from leaders. But God is gentle with our failings, especially if we are honest with Him, for He knows the layers are there.

God knew all about my pain and in a vision, drew me into a room where I was six years old. In my mind's eye, I saw a man slapping his lap in a big chair, calling me to hop up on it. His arms were reaching out to me, but I tried dodging them. He caught me, lifted me onto His lap, and spoke about how things are done for Him in ministry. I listened and nodded but started squirming and wriggling. I didn't want to be told something that'd get me run out of town and I could hear myself saying, No, no, no! The more His arms held me, the more restless I became. Suddenly, He lifted me off His lap, placed my feet onto the floor, slapped me on my rear end, pointed me to the door, and said, in a firm voice, "Off you go then, do it your way." I won that skirmish, but later understood God saw me as His ally and was pained to see me isolate myself and walk past Him, and act as if I was still an orphan.

My cohorts had no idea of the distress in the inner territory of my heart. But they did acknowledge my high-level performance as a Bible teacher, and asked me to put a curriculum together for a Bible College. After a successful couple of years of teaching Biblical theology, I was invited to lunch by four local pastors from different churches. They wanted me to begin another Bible College, this time with the idea of putting the graduating students back into those churches. I was to raise funds and build the college, which I did. I was the founding Principal yet my Sunday preaching had become very starchy. With a focus on theology, I pulled verses apart and linked them to other parts of the Bible, and the congregations welcomed this sort of teaching.

About eighteen months later, I was at home in Duffy and had just finished compiling the college program for the week ahead. Feeling happy enough with myself, I switched off my computer and sat thinking for a few quiet moments before having supper with Kath. I could hear a swift breeze brushing the tree against the window when I sensed the Lord's gentle voice. I tried to distract myself with a new book on the shelf, but His voice interrupted me.

"David, do you believe My Word?"

I glanced back at that new book and, annoyed He'd ask such a question, I had it out with God telling Him, 'Of course I believe Your word, I teach Your word and I love my job!' I tried brushing off those distressful feelings when God's voice came *again* asking me if I believed His word. Now I was losing it, and with a raised voice, said, 'You know how diligent I am at studying Your Word!' God, in a gentle tone, retorted, "Well then, what is your problem?" The wind outside had eased. In the stillness, I remembered being heartbroken and God also had not forgotten about it

Chapter 17- Ministry God's Way

either. He was upset that kids no longer heard from Him because I had stopped listening.

Very bravely, the following Sunday I openly revealed where my heart was at, with its need to please people, yet my transparency didn't go down too well. I was accused of being way to honest by those who'd rather have a scholarly explanation of the text. I boldly told them outright. 'If I believe God's Word as I say I do, then it is your heart I will want to convince.' I smiled at the taste of my own courage.

My friends knew me to be a man of high integrity. And some of these faithful friends came alongside me and taught me how to be honest in the pulpit about the ways in which God had dealt with me in the past. Being honest about my failings helped others to recognise their own struggle. I told them, 'God wants me to preach with heart and soul, instead of making my sermons spineless.'

18
Heaven on Earth

God was fed up with religion! So were some of my friends and I! The general rhetoric within the church had become so dry, and so very boring. God graciously, for He always is gracious, was about to move. He was planning on sending a fresh wind from heaven to blow and refresh weary souls. As the Principal of the Bible College, I had the responsibility of organising the midweek chapel meetings. I felt God's inner promptings.

"Dave," He said, "Put a sign *Tent of Meeting* over the chapel door." The idea is foreign to modern man, but I was rather excited, for it indicated God's intention to personally meet with us as He had done in the Old Testament.

It was a chapel morning, and I was in the middle of explaining how the sign came about. In a place packed to capacity, an overseas missionary walked in and told us of arriving the night before, and on his way to get breakfast, a vision opened up before him. In it, he saw an ordinary-looking door with *Tent of Meeting* written across the top. His wife entered the chapel and told how she had just made their bed. When she had thrown the sheet across the mattress, the words, *Tent of Meeting* appeared.

Chapter 18 Heaven on Earth

Has God told you something rather odd? Have you wished you had some confirmation about that? Both visions forever settled within my mind what God had said to me.

A few days later, God again came to me, "I will show up if you teach the students to hear My voice." Take this into a family situation, where fathers typically speak to their children. If kids know the sound of their father's voice, how much more should we, as God's children, hear our heavenly Father's voice speaking to us, as stated in John 10:27. But, the media drowns heaven's voice. If you want to hear, give yourself a break from long hours watching television, challenge any critical self-talk and feed Scriptural truth to your soul and point your focus towards heaven.

God is powerful, and some even know Him to be generous. But we modern humans are caught up in our own dynamics preventing these qualities being seen in our lives. For God to show up, we had to let go our agenda and more shockingly, our control. Our desperate need to be in control is a social construct. From the earliest age, we have been taught to organise our life according to what we want. Yet, God does not work within our frameworks. He is above them and works outside our agendas. This posed a great challenge for me, for knowing how God works, I still felt a considerable weight to fulfill the promise of His Presence.

The Boy the Tree and the Trench

Eventually, God inspired me to lead the students in a prayer, "Father, I give You permission to do with me whatever You want; however You want, wherever You want, whenever You want, with whoever You want, Amen."

From then on, in all its wonderful glory, heaven fell upon our meetings and we felt a breathtaking joy and a lightness dancing around us. People suffering longstanding illnesses were healed. Other long-awaited prayers were answered, and many fell into times of prosperity. More than it all, a tangible peace filled people's souls, and a renewed sense of meaning restored purpose to many. Happiness became a significant hallmark in relationships.

In a mighty display of God's love and power, we saw what earth would be like if we lived in the realm of heaven each day. Instead of becoming caught up in political church games, the students relinquished control and gave God the right to be who He really is–loving, kind, generous, a healer, protective, a provider and a nurturer. And a Father who lavishes abundance on His children.

19
The Hug

In the years following, God continued to display His miraculous power. But instead of being a linear account of my life, this book tracks the pathway my heart had taken.

I had everything I could want. But there was still a fair bit of self-pity around the idea of not having a father, and I still had grossly distorted pictures of God and operated from those old filters. I was struggling in the deepest part of my being with a massive disbelief about my worth as a son and a deep need to please others. I still had no idea how to bring the truth that I was valuable and cared for into my everyday experience. God was keenly aware I still had not found the Father I was looking for and the close relationship he would give me. He knew that my 'fear of man' had kept me from snuggling on His lap and that the longing was still there to have a father whisper into my ear, "I have got you, son, don't wrestle, just nestle."

Though flourishing as a Principal in a successful Bible College, my heart was still hurting. It felt sick that I had to go on in life without a loving father's strong arms around me. Overwhelmed and hopeless, I had looked for those arms in the army and searched for them in my twenty-two years working in the Australian Federal Police Force. I looked for them in my empire of wealth, hoping it would give me some significance. I had been on top of my game in the bomb squad, but still, I searched on. I searched for those arms in my doctorate and many other tertiary qualifications. But still, no matter how much I knew— and I know a fair bit, I kept searching. I had preached hundreds of sermons but would never preach about the Father. If I had, it all would have been head knowledge from textbooks. I still had trauma-related images of God as a Father, a lot of bad connotations, which had made life very confusing. When we project our broken relationships with our earthly father onto God, it's easy to say, "I don't need God to be my Father."

If you are given to striving and feel you have to give more than the next person, pray more, believe more, and generally work hard for His acceptance, then you are given to orphan ways. I had orphan patterns and orphan attitudes. My need for approval had made it impossible for me to shake off my shame. Shame makes you feel something inherently is wrong with you and demands you deliver and keep up with everyone. In a defiant willfulness to prove my worth, I demanded a great deal from myself.

Everything I believed, said, and did, had been done in my search for an identity—a name that people would recognize. To belong and to be the son of somebody was the cry of my heart. That somebody would be out there waiting for me. I sensed that.

Chapter 19 - The Hug

Vision Christian Fellowship had organised a Father's Heart conference, and over 400 people were packed inside the auditorium. It was the evening session, and the guest speaker was Jack Frost from Shiloh Ministries in America. From the pulpit, Jack confronted me with a truth I frankly didn't want to face or have confront me. It was that I had an orphan spirit. *Orphans live in orphanages.* I thought, *so move on.* Wrong. God began messing with my heart.

I was sitting in the front row with my wife feeling rather important. From the pulpit, Jack saw me, came straight to me, and put his arms around me. Instantly, I felt a spiritual Force hold me as if Heaven had invaded that space between Jack and me. He prayed, "Heavenly Father, Dave has never known what it is like to be loved by a Father like you. I ask that my arms become Your arms. Fill his heart with Your Spirit and may your love for Dave never cease." As he prayed I literally felt an intensifying of that spiritual force. Tears soaked my face. I blubbered and wept from a place so deep down that it hurt.

Jack continued praying and as he did, his voice faded and a picture came to mind, I focused on what I saw—the Father appeared and had reached down and lifted me onto His knee. With His arms around me, I heard His heart beating "I love you." Some moments are unforgettable, and some words are also–both said everything and even more than I wanted to hear. Much of my confusion dissolved.

All I ever wanted was to be hugged by my Dad. Like the prodigal, I had come home to a new beginning. I had a few new beginnings and still would have more.

It can be mighty lonely when we don't have a place in the Father's heart. I knew the church was full of orphans who did not know how much their heavenly Father loved them. I began preaching about God being our Father and saw men walk out of intense loneliness.

I formed men's groups and taught them how to become a son in the house of God. We took men away on retreats, where they experienced a torrential overflow of God's tenderhearted love. Men began to feel that same tangible expression of the Father's love that I had felt. I wanted them to be found in the forever arms of God and be nurtured in that same space of warm affection I had felt. They all came back inspired to be the fathers and husbands they wanted to become.

Though created to receive the Father's love, we cannot earn it or prove that we deserve it. God's love is freely given to us. It frees us from all fear of abandonment and rejection. The scriptures of God becoming like a Daddy to me became a reality—a hope fulfilled in my heart. I could now rest in this profound sense of security. Yet, I was still unaware of just how personal this revelation would become.

20
The Trench

The following years were extraordinarily full of unique encounters with God. But in the 2003 Canberra fires, suddenly my life was about to end. In my mind, it was over. Let's pick up the story at the time when, at an unexpected moment, the sky had turned pitch black. We were standing in an intolerable heat and darkness I had never imagined possible. Everything had vanished except for the orange flames searing the earth around us. I could not see any way of getting off that roof alive, and about to breathe my last breath, I laid on my back and prayed, 'Lord Jesus, if this is the way I am to leave the planet, I am ready. Amen.'

Moments later, Chis and I found ourselves standing in my neighbour's backyard. After that brief release into God's Hands, a fire tornado came whistling down the hill, and for a nanosecond, the sun shone through the vortex, and we could see the gutter. We took a chance, threw ourselves onto the carport roof, and then made that mighty leap into the neighbour's backyard. For over an hour, angry rage consumed everything in its path, the world had gone crazy in total payback.

While the moment was full of grief, I have learned that loss takes us to places that pleasure can never reach. With so many surrounding houses burnt to the ground, I found as many neighbours as possible and invited everyone to our smoldering ashed house for numerous support meetings. Many felt encouraged and loved.

Kath's award-winning rose garden had been totally destroyed in the fires. She, of course, was far more devastated about her roses, than everything else she had lost. Kath took to the hose and every day she gently sprinkled water onto their ashen soil. She tenderly told each black stump of their beauty and of their worth and that she was there for them.

Every day, Kath would tend her forlorn garden. Two weeks passed by when just on sunrise, she reached out and held her first bud. Her rose garden was back in full bloom! Neighbours, blocks away, walked by our house just to see the resurrected roses and smell the fragrance of new life. This showed the people of Duffy that no matter what fires come to destroy our lives, we can emerge with a brighter future.

I also had it in my heart to believe that regardless of the arrows aimed at me, God would retaliate on my behalf with good plans. In Jeremiah 29:11; *I know the thoughts I think towards you, says the Lord, thoughts of peace and not evil, to give you a future and a hope.*

God had saved my life and the life of my eldest son. We had seen many miracles, and I had preached many sermons

Chapter 20 - The Trench

on God's power and hearing His voice. I had felt His warm arms around me, significantly changing my rhetoric. I had reached great heights in my career and had become known as a wise soul, mentoring young men and women in the ways of sainthood. But still, there was an ache in my heart.

In 2004 I was praying. Prayer had become more about spending time alone with God, rather than bringing a list of things for Him to do for me. This particular day, I just wanted to enjoy heaven's delightful ambiance. While lingering in the silence, enjoying my Dad's presence, it became apparent something was still missing. A vision appeared before me. In it, I was standing in a narrow walled trench. It was cold and damp, and I felt trapped by its height. The sky was a blip above me, and there were no wall handles to help me escape or ladders on the floor. My sounds of despair filled the trench.

Suddenly a tender voice began speaking. It was so soft I had to listen carefully. "Dave, you can get out, trust Me." Then I heard a different, harsher voice, "You will never get out; you are just like your father, a failure, a drunk, and a womanizer." It was my Aunt Biddy's voice. Of course, she had always been in this trench with me. All of my life, I had felt trapped by her hellish taunts.

The gentle Voice intercepted, "You can make it out, trust Me." Hemmed in by the high walls, I focused on the gentle Voice. I did not fully believe it; I just focused on it.

The Boy the Tree and the Trench

"Dave, I am your Father and have only good for you. I will never leave you trapped in the rhetoric of your past, nor will I abandon you to it. I want you to write down for Me all the things you have voiced as a failure. Things you have started and have never finished." My Father gave me a pen and some paper. As He did, I felt His hand resting on my shoulder.

I wrote it all down.

School, family, army, police, and ministry.

He then said, "Can you see how listening to those painful words from your childhood has caused you to give up? Can you see how many other voices have trapped and ensnared you?" His gentle voice spoke again. "It's all right, and it's not your fault. You are not to blame for what people did to you. My love has never ceased despite all those events that caused you to feel a deep sense of failure and the choices you later regretted. Through it all, I have held you in My heart. You are My child – you are not orphaned, alone, or trapped but adopted into My forever eternal family. You are My precious treasure, and I love you so very much. Let it all go now, son. Trust Me, and I will get you out."

I stood in the trench, and while looking at the paper, a strange peace filled my soul. It became more evident that the floggings and nasty negative words had followed me throughout my life and had put me in a prison with "Failure,"

Chapter 20 - The Trench

written above the cell door. We can all be imprisoned with a sense of personal failure. The very idea of failure had taken up a significant place in my heart. As I agreed with the Father's version of me – that in fact, I am like Him rather than the father who abandoned me, a ladder instantly appeared. I saw my Heavenly Father standing there, calling me forth with His gentle voice. He said, "Climb out of the trench into the freedom of eternal love. I've got you, son, just nestle, don't wrestle. Under My strong wings, soar with Me." As I climbed out, I fell into His arms and was enthralled by His strength.

All my striving vanished in that beautiful moment. Being held by the Father's arms is where I live my life. In my Father's arms, I am forever His child.

> Just He and I
> In that bright glory,
> One deep joy
> shall share
> Mine to be with Him
> forever
> His that I am there.
> Author unknown.

From that moment onwards, I felt as if a colourful robe had been wrapped over my shoulders. And an inner peace beyond what I had ever known, followed me everywhere. My identity had changed entirely. I was no longer a failure but a beloved child. I was now His little boy, and often I'd sit on God's lap, celebrating my homecoming, overwhelmed at His goodness. With hope in my heart, I learned that no matter what happens, there remains a future. At various times, in my mind, I'd think things like, *Dad, thank you for leading me away from failure. What the devil meant for evil You have turned around for my good.*

Looking back, I realise I had constructed my own trench and built it with my self-beliefs and with what others said about me. God allowed me to be in that pit of failure to show He had made the way out for me. I discovered the more I moved into openness and transparency, the more apparent my Father's love became to me.

21
The Porch

A sense of self-imposed failure can trap us and leave us languishing in a deep trench. But a gentle voice from heaven, and the Father's outstretched Hand, are all we need. God didn't see me through the lens of failure. Over my lifetime, He saw me as a son in a proverbial war-zone, plying through horrendous obstacles, putting my life on the line so as to ultimately discover that I was loved and cherished. Waking up and finding my identity as a beloved son, was life-changing.

Because I had not known I was loved, I had spent all my life striving and working hard for that allusive acceptance. A world of men and women, who, like me, strain strenuously to be seen, heard and, most of all, loved. This striving needs to give way to a confidence that God utterly accepts us.

Your heavenly Father gives you and me His attention. We don't have to do a thing to get it. We don't have to perform to get it. All of His attention is available to us every second of every day. Psalm 139 alludes that even our thoughts are perceived from afar. The detail of His attention is both intimate and intricate.

The Boy the Tree and the Trench

The way back from our prodigal mindset is found sitting on God's lap, being held by Him. Spend time with the Father, become open to receiving His love. On the Father's knee, you and I can go deeper into a place of rest, and feel His loving arms around us. He is waiting for each of us. A relationship with God is built on being emotionally close. Instead of impressing God with our arduous efforts, we can release ourselves completely into His love. Nestle close into God's heart and enjoy the *soul rest* this closeness brings.

We might find it difficult to let go, especially if we have built impressive empires. Letting go takes deliberate effort. It is not easy; and only when our striving stops can we feel the love God has for us. Only then, can we all happily say, "I am a son/daughter related to the Creator of the universe."

It is such a powerful truth, one that can set you free. It set me free. This truth will bring great freedom to your soul.

There are an unfathomable number of fatherless children, all of whom are created to be sons and daughters in a tight-knit relationship with their heavenly Father. In the parable of the Prodigal Son, there are two prodigals, for neither were interested in getting close to their father. For the first part of my life, I had been striving in far away places, eating the scraps of approval. Then, unable to cope with the fallout of Vietnam, I found myself in a pigpen and longed to see the lights of home.

Chapter 21 - The Porch

Even then, the Father kept me close within His heart. At sunset, when pale apricot clouds had softened the western sky, my Father stood on His porch and, with His binoculars longingly wished to see me, waiting, year after year. Every day, He would search the horizons with His piercing eyes, and dream of my small frame. He thought of me.

The Father thinks of you. He searches the horizons and watches to see if you are on your way home. He dreams of seeing you. Yes, He honestly does. At every sunset, and every new sunrise, He watches and waits for you to make the first move. I know, when I was at Bardon resisting God at every step-of-the way He was waiting. The Father had been pruning His rose garden, when suddenly my voice came to His ears. 'I am a right nuisance, that's what I am.' Instantly, He stopped everything and, carrying a strong rose scent on His clothes, came straight to me and began drilling out all that pain in my soul. I came home, and what a homecoming I received.

But, in an equally far away place, the older brother complained about how the Father had lavished His love on me. I came under their sway and was intimidated by the older brothers in the church. Eventually, I began striving and working hard to get their approval but had become exhausted by it all. Even so, the Father knew of my desire to be close to Him, and kept me in His heart. He, in a vision, had put me on His lap and tried to talk some sense into me.

But I was more intent on pleasing the older brothers, for I had a job to do. Finally, the Father found me in the trench. He gently confronted my self-beliefs, poured oil over my wounds, and bandaged them up. It was there, in the trench, the lie, the one I had believed about myself since I was a child, was destroyed. To see my Heavenly Father's smile is enough now, and nothing else matters except His incredible love for me. I often heard myself think, *thanks Dad for rescuing me. I love You being my Dad,* and then I'd sign off ...Davey.

My story outlining my long journey into God's arms began when I had become the mirror image of the older son in the parable, dutiful, striving to impress, and complaining when others did it better than me. Then, when that had become all too much, I slipped into being like the younger son, shunning family relationships, having a great time.

I tried escaping up the tree, became stuck in the trench, and all the while, God saw the boy who just wanted his Dad to hold him.

It is time to come home. Your Father is waiting. Looking. Longing to see your face. It is time to return to your Father's house and receive His perfect love for you. A love freely given without conditions.

Postscript

Come as you are. Your name is written on the palm of God's Hand. He knows your every move and He knows the hell some of you have been through. You are loved and treasured by your Father in heaven. Bring your brokenness to Him and sit in the quietest of moments and tell God you want to know Him and be close to Him. He knows everything about you and has been waiting for you. Just let Him pour His love into your life.

Support for the way forward can be found by emailing Dave.

poultondave882@gmail.com

www.ingramcontent.com/pod-product-compliance
Lightning Source LLC
Chambersburg PA
CBHW012005090526
44590CB00026B/3885